WHAT PEOPLE ARE SAYING ABOUT THIS BOOK

A Scoutmaster holds a sacred trust. Every week, whether in the basement of the church, on the top of the mountain, or at the end of a rainy hike, the Scouts array themselves in a circle and the Scoutmaster shares with them some lessons concerning life. Sometimes the Scoutmaster will address an inspirational topic. Sometimes he will address the need for safety or cohesion on tomorrow's rappelling adventure. Maybe she will praise a Scout or a Patrol and hold up their team spirit as an exemplar for others.

No matter what, the magic of Scouting takes place while the Scouts look up in the calm of the moment and the old Scoutmaster shares his wisdom, strength, encouragement, and care for the Scouts. In his book, Scoutmaster Carpenter shares some of the finest moments from his years speaking from the heart to eager faces soaking up lessons and stories they will carry with them the rest of their lives. When the Scouts of his troop look back on their experience with the Boy Scouts of America, they will first remember Larry's heartfelt messages, which they will carry in their own hearts and pass along, in their time, to others.

Ray Capp, *Longtime Scoutmaster, Former National Order of the Arrow Chairman, and member of the BSA National Executive Board*

Serving as a District Executive for the Occoneechee Council in Raleigh, North Carolina, I met Larry Carpenter, a thirteen-year-old Scout in Troop 357. Larry went on to become an Eagle Scout. When Explorer Post 5 sponsored by WRAL-TV was formed in 1969, he joined this Explorer Post.

As Camp Director of Camp Durant in 1970 and 1972, I hired Larry to work in our camp kitchen and dining hall. He went on to work on the council camp staff for nine additional years. However, my greatest thrill was attending the National Explorer Presidents' Congress in Washington, DC in 1975 and seeing Larry elected as the National Explorer President. It was very exciting to see President Gerald Ford install Larry on the White House lawn with other Explorers and adult leaders attending the Congress.

I could readily see that Larry was a natural born leader and he went on to serve Scouting in countless ways. This book is a prime example of his service and commitment. While I never had the chance to see Larry in action as a Scoutmaster, I am certain his Scoutmaster's Minutes were rewarding and inspiring for his young Scouts. This book will enable other Scoutmasters to share these same great Scoutmaster's Minutes with their Scouts at their weekly Scout meetings.

J. Rex Thomas, *Former District Executive, Member of Council Board of Directors, and Commercial Real Estate Executive*

I met Larry Carpenter in 1975 during the BSA's National Explorer Presidents' Congress. He was a contender for National President and was elected by over 2,000 young adults in attendance from all over the USA. He gave outstanding leadership that year, and I wasn't surprised to learn that he was also an Eagle Scout. The motto he learned in that process was "Be Prepared." Scoutmasters and others in leadership positions are called upon to provide sound counsel to their members at every meeting, which can sometimes be a challenge. *Minute by Minute: A Collection of 100 of the Best Scoutmaster's Minutes* is just what you've been looking for. Larry gives us an excellent collection of "minutes" in support of Scouting goals.

John Oaks Thurston, *Retired Scout Executive*

Larry and I have known each other since our teenage Exploring years in the 1970s. But I haven't kept up with the experience that Larry accumulated as a unit leader of Troops and Crews. I like the way he has compiled this collection of inspirational minutes using the Scout Oath and Law as the organizational framework making it easy for the rest of us to use. I also appreciate how his minutes take a broad interpretation of each of the elements. The stories he relates make us think about how to apply what could be viewed as narrow concepts such as trustworthy, loyal, helpful, and friendly into a wider view of what it is to live as a Scout in everyday life. Larry makes the words we have taught for over 100 years come alive in our actions, "words to live by!"

Richard A. Davies, *Former National Explorer President and CEO of Greater New York Councils*

Minute by Minute

A Collection of 100 of the Best Scoutmaster's Minutes

Larry Carpenter

Clovercroft Publishing

Minute by Minute: A Collection of 100 of the Best Scoutmaster's Minutes

Published by Clovercroft Publishing, Franklin, Tennessee

All capitalizations in this book are consistent with those standards set by the Boy Scouts of America, as outlined in the *The Language of Scouting* and *BSA Style Manual,* Revised February 2020, on the Scouting website at https://www.scouting.org/resources/los/.

Edited by David Brown

Cover and Interior Design by Suzanne Lawing

Printed in the United States of America

978-1-954437-00-5

DEDICATION

This book is dedicated to my wife, Linda. Not only did she make my life a blessing, but she had the patience to put up with all my Scouting adventures!

ACKNOWLEDGEMENT

Many people encouraged me in the writing of this book. The first person who comes to mind was my late mother. As my Den Mother, she encouraged me to join Cub Scouts, initiating my life-long love for Scouts. My late father was always an encouragement, too. Especially when he smuggled some of Mom's sausage to us on the coldest campout I ever went on!

My first Scoutmaster, when we lived in Tallahassee, Florida while my dad was getting his PhD, was Melvin Pope. He introduced me to the joy of the outdoors. My second Scoutmaster was Sergeant Pate. His first name was Joel, but we just called him Sarge.

I remember him having to drive me home from a camping trip. I think I had a Pee Wee football game. He asked me how I was liking Scouts. He actually knew my rank and my position in the troop. I remember thinking, "Wow, this guy really knows who I am and actually cares how I turn out. I'm liking this Scouting program!"

My third Scoutmaster, when we moved back to Raleigh, North Carolina, Joel Reames, was the toughest Scoutmaster in the world. I'm pretty sure that's listed in the *Guinness World Records* book. He flunked me in Cooking merit badge four times! I know I deserved it, as I'm a lousy cook. But Mr. Reames knew that life is hard and part of his role as a Scoutmaster was to prepare me to be a success.

My Explorer Post Advisor was Powell Kidd. Powell Kidd was truly the coolest guy I ever knew. It's safe to say that I patterned my Scout adult leadership style after Powell. Rex Thomas was the first District Executive I ever worked with as he hired me to work in the kitchen at Camp Durant when I was thirteen. Later in my career, Rex is the one who encouraged me to run for Area III Explorer Chairman. When the guy who won decided he couldn't serve, Rex Thomas was the guy who called the Southeast Region Vice President, Scott Sorrels, and convinced him to skip over the second place candidate and go with the guy who came in third. That would be me. Speaking of Scott, he's the guy who taught me how to be a good manager and executive. And he's the guy who talked me in to running for National Explorer President. He remains one of my best friends in Scouting.

Bob Lilley was my Order of the Arrow Dance Team Advisor. The sacrifices that Bob made to build our dance team and instill in us an appreciation of Native Americans was one of the highlights of my youth. I still remember the tears in Bob's eyes when we stepped off the bus after returning from winning the National Dance Team Championship at the National Order of the Arrow Conference in Santa Barbara, California. I always made it a point to treat my Dance Team members in my local OA chapter to a meal after every performance, as I always remember Bob taking us to Shoney's, where he would ask the waitress, "Got any chili in the pot, Honey?"

This book wouldn't have been possible without the editing skills of David Brown. And Suzanne Lawing was a joy to work with in the cover and interior design. I hope that I didn't drive both of them crazy and they will help me with the next book!

FOREWORD

Where do we find men and women, all servant leaders, who agree to serve as Scoutmasters or unit leaders for their local community? It takes a measure of selflessness and commitment to a cause, without ever asking anything in return. The volunteer payday may not come until years later, at an Eagle Court of Honor, perhaps, or just hearing about the success and happiness of one of your Scouts so many years later. Often leading by example, or sometimes by offering a well-timed piece of advice, the impact that a unit leader can have on a young Scout's life is hard to measure, but always present.

Sometimes that advice can be found in the Scoutmaster's Minute, that moment at the end of the troop meeting where you give the Scouts something to think about until your next time together. It need not be a lecture, could often be a spontaneous thought, but sometimes it can benefit from a little preparation and forethought.

I enjoyed reading Larry Carpenter's new book, *Minute by Minute*, a collection of Scoutmaster Minutes. The book is a wonderful collection of short but impactful messages, all well researched and often based on the real life success stories of people who made a difference in their own lives. Minute by Minute provides a ready reference for every new and seasoned Scoutmaster. True to the Boy Scout motto, Be Prepared, this wonderful collection will provide you with a ready reference of thoughtful and inspiring messages, all grounded in the Scout Oath and Law, that you can use with your Scouts.

Larry Carpenter, himself a Scoutmaster of many years, brings a wealth of Scout experience to his assembly of Scoutmaster Minutes. I have known Larry since we were in our teens, serving together as national officers of the Exploring program of the Boy Scouts of America. Larry quickly surfaced as a national youth leader, and I watched with pride from the lawn of the White House as President Ford welcomed Larry as the new National Explorer President. His journey as a servant leader was only starting at that point, and no one could have imagined the rich and rewarding time that we have enjoyed together.

I hope that you enjoy *Minute by Minute*, and trust that it will become a well-read book on your Scoutmaster bookshelf as you pursue your own journey on the Scouting trail.

Scott Sorrels
National Commissioner
Boy Scouts of America

INTRODUCTION

Having served six years as a Scoutmaster and another four years as a Venture Crew Advisor, I learned that one of the most intimidating tasks is the Scoutmaster's Minute. At the end of every meeting, the Scoutmaster faces the task of giving a brief closing message to the Scouts. It can be motivating, inspirational, educational, and is, hopefully, entertaining. That's a lot of pressure. Not every Scoutmaster has the knowledge, resources, creativity, or talent to come up with approximately fifty Scoutmaster's Minutes every year.

Additionally, we know that the number one fear of people is speaking in public. While we can assume that someone who chooses to become a Scoutmaster probably has this skill mastered, if a Scoutmaster is not sure that what they have to say is interesting or informative, they will definitely be a little nervous.

As a lifetime public speaker, the writing of Scoutmaster's Minutes came pretty easily to me. Every time I looked at my binder full of hundreds of Scoutmaster's Minutes, I kept thinking that I should put these to good use and share them with other Scoutmasters. This book is the result of that process.

I decided to organize the Minutes by topic. Included in the book are five Minutes for each point of the Scout Law. There are two Minutes for each of the points of the Scout Oath. Next, I included two Minutes each on the Scout motto and the Scout slogan. Those are followed by eighteen Minutes on various topics including honesty, motivation, leadership, and other important topics.

With one hundred Minutes, you have the next two years of meetings covered. After that, once you get the hang of how the Scoutmaster's Minutes work, I hope that you can come up with many more Scoutmaster's Minutes. If not, I am already working on Volume 2!

Feel free to use the motivational and inspirational topics in your business, social networking posts, and any other times that they apply. But, if nothing else, I hope that the stories and messages contained within this book make that weekly Scoutmaster's Minute a little less daunting!

Larry Carpenter

A SCOUT IS TRUSTWORTHY #1

A LACK OF TRUST PUTS YOU IN A CELL

One of the greatest writers of the twentieth century was Graham Greene. He once said, "It is impossible to go through life without trust. That is to be imprisoned in the worst cell of all, oneself." You all know what to be imprisoned means. It means you are locked up all by yourself with no one to talk to and nobody to laugh with. Your freedom to play games is restricted. You can't just go to a movie or hang out with your friends. It's not a good place to be.

Graham Greene says that not trusting anyone is like being in prison. But it's a different type of prison than the one with cells and bars. It's like being imprisoned within yourself. You are surrounded by lots of people who you could talk to, laugh with, and cry with. But it's like they aren't there for you. Why? Because you don't trust them. You are scared to tell them things. You think that they will betray you and tell your secrets to other people. In order to avoid this, we must learn to trust others.

But there is a funny thing about trusting others. Before you can trust others, you must first learn to be trusted yourself. This is what the Scout Law means by saying that we must be trustworthy. If you break the word trustworthy down into its pieces, you realize that it means that you must be worthy of their trust.

What does that mean? Well, people assign worth to everything that they do or come into contact with. We have limited time in life. So, we mentally assign a value to everything. If something is important to us, we give it a high value. If it isn't important to us, we assign a low value to it. I'm not talking about physically assigning a value to it. Like placing a sticker with the price on it onto everything and everyone we come into contact with. But, it's a mental value.

Let's say that one of you likes to go to science fiction movies. If a trailer for a new science fiction movie comes out, you place a high value to it. You might stop everything else you are doing in order to watch it. But if you would prefer to read mystery novels, you would assign a low value to the movie trailer. You wouldn't drop everything you were doing in order to watch the trailer.

Well, that's how trusting others works. If someone watches the way you live your life and they decide that you can't be trusted, they assign a low value to having a friendship with you. But if they decide that you can be trusted, they assign a very high value to their relationship with you. In other words, you are worthy of their trust!

Take a good hard look at yourself. Can you be trusted? Are you worthy of that trust? And, if so, can you trust other people?

A SCOUT IS TRUSTWORTHY #2

ALWAYS BE WHERE YOU ARE SUPPOSED TO BE

One of the greatest boxers of all time was Jim Corbett. His nickname was Gentleman Jim Corbett. He was the world heavyweight champion from 1892 to 1897. With the nickname of Gentleman Jim, you know he must have been a nice guy. Until he got in the boxing ring!

Gentleman Jim once said: "You become a champion by fighting one more round. When things are tough, you fight one more round."

Obviously, Gentleman Jim's advice on becoming a champion was that you could not give up. No matter how much pain he was in as a boxer, he still had to answer the bell. After all, if you don't answer the bell, and get back in the boxing match, you can't become the champion.

But there is another meaning in what Gentleman Jim said. One of the Scout Laws is that we are to be trustworthy. When we say that someone is trustworthy, we usually mean that they are honest. That they can be trusted. If we tell them something in confidence, we can feel secure that they will not share it with someone else.

But there's another aspect of being trustworthy. And that is that we can be trusted to be where we are supposed to be when we are supposed to be there. Gentleman Jim was supposed to be in the ring. His fans knew that when the bell rang, they could be confident that Gentleman Jim would come off of his stool and be prepared to battle.

Life is similar to that. When was the last time that someone promised you to be somewhere, but they didn't show? Do you remember how you felt at that point? You felt like you had been misled. Maybe you felt like you had been betrayed. Or maybe even it was so serious that you felt like you had been lied to.

When was the last time you told someone else that you would be somewhere, but you weren't there when it counted? Now think of how they must have felt. It's not a good feeling. Gentleman Jim told us that a champion can be counted upon to be where they are supposed to be, always coming back to finish that athletic event. In order for us to be trustworthy, we need to do the same. If we tell someone that we are going to be somewhere or do something, then we need to keep our word. We need for them to be able to trust that we are going to live up to our word.

A SCOUT IS TRUSTWORTHY #3

WE MUST RIGHT THE WRONGS

At the end of the nineteenth century and the early twentieth century, people of color in the United States were battling for their rights. One of the earliest civil rights leaders was Ida B. Wells. She was a newspaper journalist. She fought for the rights of African Americans. She was one of the early founders of the NAACP. She once said: "The way to right wrongs is to turn the light of truth upon them."

What she was referring to was the wrongs that had been done against African American people. It started with slavery. But even after the slaves were free, Blacks found it very difficult to vote, hold jobs, or even use the same facilities as whites. As a journalist, she used her newspaper articles to shine the light on bad practices of the time. She felt that getting the stories out in the open would be what would cause people to change the way things were done.

There are a lot of wrong things in the world. As a Scout, it is our duty to point out these wrongs so that they can be changed. One of the points of the Scout Law is that a Scout is trustworthy. But what does shining a light on a wrong have to do with being trustworthy? Well, have you ever heard the term "aids and abets?" Or have you ever heard of someone who is referred to as an accessory to a crime? What both of these mean is that the person in question isn't the one who committed the actual crime. But they are still guilty of a crime. For example, someone might rob a bank. But then, the driver of the getaway car meets them and helps them to escape. Did the driver rob the bank? No. But according to our law, has the getaway driver committed a crime? Certainly.

In our lives, we might witness something that is seriously wrong. It's easy to simply look the other way. But being trustworthy means that we can be trusted to do the right thing. In this case, the right thing would be to report the crime to someone of authority.

Our society is composed of millions of people who must work together in order to make our society a success. We must be trusted to do the right thing. We must also be trusted to make sure that others are doing the right thing. The next time you see that someone has done something that is seriously wrong, make sure to shine the light on it. Be a trustworthy Scout, who doesn't allow a crime to go unpunished.

A SCOUT IS TRUSTWORTHY #4

STAYING WHERE YOU ARE

Grandpa and Grandma were out for a drive. They pulled up behind a young couple in the car ahead of them. Grandma noticed that the young woman was sitting in the middle of the seat up against the young man. She said to Grandpa, "You know, we used to sit that close together." Grandpa said, "I'm still sitting in the same place I always have."

Sometimes, we move away from people or things. Sometimes, we move away from beliefs or morals with which we started off our lives. Often, these moves are so subtle or happen over so long a time that we don't even notice them. One day, we wake up and we wonder why someone is no longer our friend. Or we notice that we don't enjoy doing something that we used to enjoy. Or we now feel that something that we used to think was wrong ... Well, we just don't think it's that bad anymore.

One of the Scout Laws is that a Scout is to be trustworthy. There are lots of things that go into being trustworthy. But one of the most important things is that, in order to be trustworthy, you have to be constant and consistent.

Do you have friends that seem to change all of the time? Their behavior changes constantly. Sometimes, they are in a good mood, the best friend you could have. But the next day, they are sad or moody. They are very hard to be around. Their emotions always seem to be on a roller coaster. They are unpredictable. They always have to have drama in their lives. Sometimes, it's a real challenge just to be around them.

Now, imagine you had to trust them to do something really important. Or you needed to confide in them a big secret. With their erratic behavior, are you comfortable in trusting them?

Well, the same thing is true for you. People want to place their trust in someone who is consistent, down-to-earth, and predictable. They want to know that what they see is what they get.

So, if you want people to feel like you are trustworthy, save the drama for the school play. Think and act consistently and stably.

A SCOUT IS TRUSTWORTHY #5

LET PEOPLE KNOW THAT THEY CAN BE TRUSTED

Booker T. Washington was one of the leading intellectuals of his time. During the late 1800s, he became an author, educator, founder of the Tuskegee Institute, and an advisor for multiple presidents. Other smart people can make similar claims. But what made Booker T. Washington so unique was how he did it. He was born into slavery in the South, prior to the Civil War. He overcame this humble beginning, taught himself when an education was not generally available for African Americans, and rose to become one of the most intellectual people in the United States.

Booker T. Washington once said: "Few things can help an individual more than to place responsibility on him, and to let him know that you trust him."

We don't know who first told Booker T. Washington that he could be trusted. But I'm guessing that early in his childhood, more than one person told him that he could be trusted. How did this affect him? Well, you have it in his own words.

What do you do when you're handed something valuable? It may be your mother asking you to hold her ring while she puts cream on her hands. It may be your teacher asking you to carry your class's school project into the science fair. Or, it may just be your best friend asking you to hang onto both of your clothes while you put on your swimsuits. But whatever it is of value that you are asked to hold onto, do you just handle it casually like you might hold a cold drink? No. If you're asked to hold something of value, you handle it gingerly. You don't let it out of your sight. You pick it up carefully and you put it back down again carefully.

Well, according to Booker T. Washington, responsibility is sort of like that. When someone hands you responsibility, you take care of it. You do the right thing. You want to make sure that the responsibility that you have been given is not misplaced.

Trust is only given to you if you handle that responsibility with utmost care. But look carefully at what Booker T. Washington said. It's not enough that we are given responsibility. It is also important that we are told that we can be trusted. Doesn't it feel great when someone tells you that you can be trusted? At that point, we know that we are truly living up to the Scout Law, a Scout is trustworthy.

But finally, it's a two-way street. You feel great when someone gives you responsibility and tells you that you can be trusted. But, wouldn't it be nice to share that great feeling with someone else? The next time that you have someone that you can trust, let them know. It's a great feeling to be trusted and to be able to trust others.

A SCOUT IS LOYAL #1

ABE'S DOG, FIDO

Have you ever wondered where some of the most popular dog names come from? Some of them are pretty obvious. A dog named Spot probably has that as a distinguishing feature. Dogs get human names like Butch all the time. But there's one popular dog name that I bet you don't know where it comes from.

I'm talking about the name Fido. Lots of people name their dog Fido, but they don't know where it comes from. It's an interesting story.

The dog name Fido came from Abe Lincoln. The origin of the word is Latin for "to trust or confide in." It's the same origin of the word fidelity, which means to be loyal. Lincoln suffered from bouts of depression. He found that the loyalty that he saw in his dog raised his spirits. When people heard the story, they began naming their dogs Fido.

While none of us knows very much about Lincoln's dog, Fido, I bet that there are several things about him that we can assume to be true. First, Fido was probably waiting anxiously when Abe came home from work. His little tail was probably wagging. He might've been jumping up and down. In other words, he couldn't wait to see his master.

When Honest Abe needed a friendly ear, Fido was probably right there for him. Even if he could've talked, I doubt he would have said something like, "Hold that thought, Abe. I need to finish reading this book." No, when Abe needed attention, Fido probably dropped everything he was doing and listened with all of his attention.

And when Abe was feeling a little depressed, Fido probably undertook it as his mission to cheer him up. He might've danced around and done something funny. He might have picked up a stick and encouraged Abe to give it a throw. He might have licked Abe's hands. He would have done almost anything to cheer up his owner.

This is what loyalty is all about. One of the Scout Laws is that a Scout is loyal. It's one of those Scout Laws that is easy to say, but harder to do. We have always heard that we should be loyal to our friends, our family, and others. But what exactly does that mean? The loyalty or fidelity that Fido showed for Abraham Lincoln gives us several good examples. First, when a friend or family member comes into your presence, welcome them as the friend that they are. Don't be afraid to give a handshake, a hug, a nod of the head, or a word of greeting.

Second, when a friend or relative needs your attention, give it to them. Hey, you can always come back to that book or television show. Loyalty means dropping what you're doing, becoming engaged with them, and giving them your full attention.

Third, loyalty to your friends and family means to be there to support them when they most urgently need your support. In times of loss, fear, or just when they're feeling a little low, a loyal friend is always there for someone else. Next time you're with your friends, remember Abraham Lincoln's little dog, Fido. Be loyal to your friends, like Fido was for honest Abe.

A SCOUT IS LOYAL #2

THE MARINES ARE ALWAYS THERE FOR EACH OTHER

Can anybody tell me what is the motto of the United States Marines? If you said Semper Fidelis or Semper Fi, you got it. But what does that mean? It comes from Latin. And it means simply always faithful. On one level, that could seem like a strange motto for a group of tough Marines. Always faithful, sounds like what a husband or wife might send their spouse for their twenty-fifth anniversary! But in the old days, faithful had a broader meaning.

Let's take a look at the origin of the word. This one is pretty easy. Faithful, when broken down, simply means full of faith. Again, that phrase may seem strange to describe the members of the Marine Corps. Full of faith sounds like a religious person.

But faith in someone means that you believe in them. You support them. You're always there for them. Someone who is full of faith stands firmly behind someone else. If you are always faithful, you do this, well, all of the time.

Let's put the meaning of always faithful into some modern wording. You have all heard the phrase, "I've got your back." Now, that definitely comes with some military connotations.

As you know, when a soldier is on the battlefield, the most dangerous place for them is immediately behind them. Therefore, if someone "has their back," it means that they have their back covered. They don't need to be worried about an enemy coming up behind them.

But watching someone else's back requires the ultimate in loyalty. Why, because if we are watching their back, who's watching our back? By adopting the motto Semper Fidelis, the Marines were saying that everybody in their organization was watching everybody else's back.

Here's an example of how that works. In the early wars between England and Scotland, one of the most feared things for an English soldier was when the Scottish troops charged at them with their broadswords. Broadswords could come down with such force that it could easily split the English soldier's head, even when wearing a helmet. The only defense that the English soldier had was to stab the oncoming Scottish soldier with his lance. But the Scottish soldiers also carried a large shield. When held directly in front of them, the English soldier had nowhere to stab the Scotsman with his lance.

But at the Battle of Culloden, in 1746, the English commander came up with a different strategy. He noticed that when a Scottish soldier had his shield out in front of him, the only way to get the lance behind the shield so that it could pierce the soldier was to jab sideways. So, instead of each of the soldiers using his lance to stab the Scottish soldier in front of them, they would stab the soldier in front of the English soldier to their left. That takes a lot of nerve. You really had to rely on your fellow soldier not just to have your back, but also to have your front! But the strategy worked. The soldiers were faithful and loyal to their fellow soldiers. Enough of them put their life at risk to protect the soldier standing beside them, and the English army won the battle.

Let's hope that the next time your buddy needs your help, it doesn't put your life at risk. But like the Marines, a good Scout is always faithful. He or she is loyal to their buddies and always has their back.

A SCOUT IS LOYAL #3

THE WAY THAT GEESE FLY

Have you ever looked up in the sky as geese fly over and wondered why they fly in formation? Well, scientists have studied this. What they have found is that geese fly in formation for two primary reasons. First, is wind resistance. Geese fly for incredible distances. When Canadian geese decide that it's too cold in Canada, they head south.

As they fly, one of the things that makes them the most tired is having to fly against the wind. If you've ever stood outside on a windy day, you know how much force the wind can have. But even if it isn't windy, but just normal weather, flying or moving into the wind leads to what is called wind resistance. Have you ever watched runners run a long-distance race? The runners get up close behind the runner in front of them. It's called drafting. The runner who is ahead of them is having to plow their way through the air and the wind resistance that it offers. The runner who is behind the lead runner is able to save energy and choose the right moment to burst out from behind the other runner to the finish line.

That's what the geese are doing. They don't line up one after another. That would lead to a huge difference in endurance. The goose at the front would get really tired, while the goose at the back would be much more energetic. Instead, they arrange themselves in a V formation. This means that each goose is experiencing an almost equal amount of wind resistance. But the lead goose is still getting the worst of it. So, what the geese do is they rotate. One goose might take the lead for a while, then be replaced by another goose, who is then replaced by another goose.

The second reason that geese fly in formation is in order to communicate with each other and to keep track of all of the birds. If the birds were in a line, and the goose at the end of the line was having difficulties, was attacked, or for any other reason had an issue, the birds in line ahead of that goose might not know it. But by flying in a V formation, the geese are able to communicate with each other and to keep an eye on each other. If one of the birds is having a difficulty, one of the other birds will quickly spot it.

What can we learn from the V formation of the geese? One of the Scout Laws is that a Scout is loyal. Loyalty means that you place the needs of others ahead of your own needs. If the geese were too concerned about their own needs, they would simply focus on their own needs while flying. But their formation means that they communicate and keep track of each other. They make sure that their fellow geese don't get too tired. In other words, they are loyal to each other.

The next time you are with a friend, be loyal. Think of the V formation of the geese and how it encourages them to think of the needs of others and to be aware of their needs.

A SCOUT IS LOYAL #4

FRODO AND SAM

One of the most popular book series of all times is *The Lord of the Rings* series by J.R.R. Tolkien. If you haven't read it, I highly recommend it. The movie series was one of the highest grossing movie series of all times.

Several factors contributed to the enormous success of the book. The book took place in Middle-earth, with its exotic locations. The constant action in the books was another factor contributing to its success. Many sleepless nights were spent as readers could not put the book down.

But I think one of the reasons that the book was so successful was the story of camaraderie and loyalty. A group of total strangers banded together to fight against the threat to the world. An incredible loyalty sprung up among the different characters as they looked out for each other.

But perhaps the strongest example of loyalty was between the two main characters, the Hobbits named Frodo and Sam. Sam was the manservant for Frodo. His job was to take care of his master. It is not uncommon for someone who serves or works for another person to feel a strong sense of loyalty. But the loyalty of Sam for Frodo went far beyond the loyalty that an employee has for their company. Here's a line from Sam that describes his loyalty for Frodo. To put the line in context, Sam was not able to hold the ring that Frodo had and was attempting to destroy. Many people would have simply said, "Well, there's nothing I can do to help." Or, "That's not my job." Or, "That's his problem, not mine."

But not Frodo. Here's what he said about the ring: "Come, Mr. Frodo!' he cried. 'I can't carry it for you, but I can carry you and it as well. So up you get! Come on, Mr. Frodo dear! Sam will give you a ride. Just tell him where to go, and he'll go."

One of the Scout Laws is a Scout is loyal. Loyalty can be shown in many ways. But I think that the loyalty that you read for Sam can best be described as the ultimate in loyalty. Many of us might show loyalty for our company, a friend, our school, or a person of authority simply because that is what society expects of us. But, when the going gets rough, that loyalty quickly dissolves.

On the other hand, the ultimate loyalty goes beyond what is simply expected of us. It is the willingness to stand beside someone or something even when the going gets tough. Just like Frodo, when an easily shown loyalty goes away, we should look for creative ways to remain loyal. Frodo couldn't pick up the ring, but he could pick up Frodo while he was still holding the ring. That's the type of creative solution one needs to show in the ultimate loyalty.

Next time the going gets rough, don't just immediately throw in the towel. If you are truly loyal to someone or something, think hard about creative ways that you can still help them out. That's the type of true loyalty of which the Scout Law is speaking.

A SCOUT IS LOYAL #5

THE POWER OF THE GROUP

You can have a long and great debate over who was the greatest American president. But inevitably, almost any list you look at will always have Franklin D. Roosevelt in the top five. Why? Roosevelt was president during two of the most trying times in American history. First, he came to the presidency after the start of the Great Depression. While historians will argue over how effective his program called The New Deal was, there is a general consensus that the optimism and uplifting tone that President Roosevelt set was instrumental in helping our country to recover.

But if that wasn't eventful enough, President Roosevelt was our president when we entered into World War II, the largest conflict our world has ever seen. Again, historians can argue over the effectiveness of Roosevelt's wartime strategy. But, again, no one can deny that President Roosevelt's optimism and upbeat nature gave our country hope during some of its darkest days.

President Roosevelt once said: "People acting together as a group can accomplish things which no individual acting alone could ever hope to bring about."

There are certain things in life where people operate better as an individual. You better not have somebody helping you on your college aptitude test or you're going to get into a lot of trouble! There are sports, such as golf and tennis, where you have to compete by yourself. In some sports, if you receive any type of coaching or advice from someone else, you can be penalized. But in most sports, you participate as a team. In school, even if you must take tests by yourself, the best environment for learning is still considered to be as part of a classroom full of people. There are a few businesses where someone works by themselves. But in most businesses, the best companies operate together as a team.

Why is it, as President Roosevelt stated, that we tend to operate best as a team? Well, with many things in life, you don't have all of the answers. Let's say that you are on a trivia team. You might be really good at knowing movies, but what if they ask a trivia question about history? Wouldn't it be good to have someone with that knowledge on your team? In athletics, if you were on the football team, and you're good at passing the ball, isn't it good to also have someone who can kick the ball, or block, or guard the opposing wide receiver? If you are a cheerleader, it's awful tough to form a tower with just yourself!

So, I think we will all agree that teamwork is important. But what is one of the most important characteristics of a successful team? Loyalty. One of the Scout Laws is that a Scout is loyal. Loyalty in Scouting is important, but it's important in every team effort that we undertake. Let's go back to that cheerleading squad. Do you want to be the one they are throwing up in the air if the person at the base isn't fully loyal and committed to what the team is trying to do?

Remember that a team of committed individuals is always going to be stronger than that individual all by themselves. But in order to create that successful team, it is critical that each and every member is loyal to each and every other member of the team.

A SCOUT IS HELPFUL #1

A LIMITED AMOUNT OF TIME

Can you name something that only a dozen or fewer people have done all throughout history? It's kind of hard to do. But here's one that you will all be familiar with. Guess how many men have walked upon the face of the moon? If you said twelve, you got it right. But can you tell me who was the first man to walk on the moon? If you were paying attention in history class, you will remember that it was a man named Neil Armstrong.

When Neil Armstrong returned from the moon, he said that one of the hardest things for him to do was to determine what to do next. After all, how do you follow an act such as walking on the face of the moon? But he went on to live a life of service to others. And as he decided on the types of things that he wanted to do, he made a very interesting statement. He said, "I believe every human has a finite number of heartbeats. I don't intend to waste any of mine."

Here's something to think about. At the moment you were born, you could have gone into Guinness World Records. What for? Well, for one brief moment, you were the youngest person on the face of the earth! But the moment you were born, a clock started ticking. And according to that clock, you have a finite number of seconds that you will live.

So, the question becomes, what are you going to do with that time? You could devote all of that time to yourself. But there's a good word that summarizes people who devote all of their time to themselves. That word is selfish.

What, then, is the alternative? Devote much of that time to others. There's a word for that also. And that word is helpful.

According to the Scout Law, a Scout is helpful. If we decide that our seconds here on earth should be devoted to helping others, what do we need to do? Well, first, you have to look around for ways to help others. Sometimes, these opportunities will be obvious as we see people in need of help. But other times, it can be more subtle. After all, people don't always like to ask for help. They fear that it makes them look weak. You might have heard the phrase, "I don't want any charity." What these people are saying is that they don't want a handout. They want to be able to do everything on their own. So, sometimes, you have to look around for people who are in need.

Once you identify their need, you have to figure out a way to help them. It's not always as easy as just giving them some money or writing them a check. Oftentimes, money isn't the solution. We have to give of our time. We might have to give of our knowledge. After all, there are a lot of ways to offer help.

The next time you find that you have some spare time on your hands, remember that those seconds are actually very precious. You can never get them back. So, as astronaut Neil Armstrong advised us, make use of that spare time to give help to someone in need.

A SCOUT IS HELPFUL #2

GIVE WITH JOY

Leo Buscaglia was an author known as Dr. Love. He wrote motivational and inspirational books that encouraged people to love one another more than they loved themselves. One of his most famous quotes was, "Only when we give joyfully, without hesitation or thought of gain, can we truly know what love means."

When most people think of love, they think of falling head over heels for that special someone in their life. At your age, it would be your boyfriend or girlfriend. Later in life, it could be your spouse. If we carry love a little bit further, it would be the feeling we have for members of our family. Unfortunately, many people don't carry the concept of love out any further than that. But if you look at the beliefs of virtually any religion, they all have the concept of loving one another. Love for your fellow man means to respect them, be kind to them, show courtesy to them, stand up for them, and consider their interests in addition to our own interests.

Like many things in life, that's easy to say, but harder to do. Mr. Buscaglia gives us a good place to start. He tells us that we should give joyfully, without hesitation or thought of gain. What kind of things might we give to others? Well, the first thing that comes to mind is money. I would encourage all of you to give charitably to organizations that serve others and people who are less fortunate. We can give our time and efforts to people or organizations. We can give our advice to someone. We can give our knowledge to someone.

But I don't think Mr. Buscaglia was saying that this simple act of giving, alone, gives us joy. What he was saying was that we should give JOYFULLY. Here's the distinction. Have you ever seen a movie or a television show where a rich person was asked to give money to a charity or some other cause? They simply pull out the checkbook and write a check, with no emotion or involvement. The amount that they are giving is probably a small, insignificant amount of their total worth. But the point is that they are simply giving. They are not giving joyfully.

When you give of yourself to others, make sure that it meets the two criteria that Mr. Buscaglia provided. Make sure that you are giving it without hesitation. Make sure that you are giving it because you feel it's the right thing to do and it brings joy to you to be able to do it. But also, do not do it with a thought of the gain in mind. Don't be thinking, "Hey, I'm going to give this money so that I can get something back in return of even greater value." The value that you get for your giving is the joy that you feel and the joy that you pass on to someone else.

One of the Scout Laws is that a Scout is helpful. Giving to others is a great way to be helpful. But the next time you decide to help someone by giving to them, make sure that you are giving joyfully. It's a great way to show your love for others!

A SCOUT IS HELPFUL #3

BUT I WAS JUST TRYING TO BE HELPFUL

Have you ever heard yourself having to say, "But I was just trying to be helpful!"? Sometimes, you have to say that phrase if you did something that you shouldn't have or things just went frightfully wrong. For example, let's say that you were trying to clean your room. But as you picked up your clothes from the floor, that half-drunk drink from the night before spilled over the carpet. When Mom or Dad came into the room and asked you how you spilt the drink, your first comment would probably be, "But I was just trying to be helpful!"

But there's another time when we might make that statement. And it comes when we are truly confused about why our offer of help was rebuffed.

One of the greatest boxers of all time is Mike Tyson. He actually is the youngest heavyweight champion of all time. Mike Tyson once said, "Everyone has a plan until they get punched in the face."

Like all good athletes, Mike Tyson would always come into a fight with a plan. He would've watched hours of video of his opponent, trying to figure out what were his strengths and weaknesses. Then, he would draw up a plan to avoid his opponent's strengths and attack his weaknesses.

But what Mike Tyson was saying is that everything doesn't always go according to plan. In the boxing ring, it you're getting pummeled by your opponent, it's tough to stay with your original plan!

Well, that's a lot like it is in life. You may have noticed that one of your friends needs help. You're a good Scout. You remember that one of the Scout Laws is a Scout is helpful. So, you develop a plan to help them out. It may involve loaning them some money or helping them to earn some money. Maybe you help them understand their schoolwork. Or you explain something to them so that they don't continue to make the same error over and over.

But what can sometimes happen when you attempt to be helpful? Sometimes, your friends just don't want your help. They may say things like: "Hey, I don't need your charity." Or even more cruelly, they might say "Hey, if I need your help, I'll ask for it."

So, how do you handle that? Well first, remember that your friend is in a difficult situation. Their emotions are probably running high. They may even be desperate. When people are desperate and emotions are running high, they don't always say things that they mean. So, first, chill out. Don't take what they say personally.

Next, show some persistence. In order for you to help your friend, you may just need to wear them down. Just because they rebuked you with your first offer of help doesn't mean that you don't make that offer again. Give them a chance to settle down. Then, calmly approach them again. You might need to say something like, "Hey, I didn't mean to hurt your feelings. I'm just trying to help."

But whether your offer of help is accepted the first time, after repeated requests, or has to be taken off the table, as a good Scout and a friend, always be there to help your friends in need.

A SCOUT IS HELPFUL #4

HOW TO SOLVE A PROBLEM

One of the greatest jazz performers of all time was Duke Ellington. But not only was Duke Ellington known for his talent, he was also known as one who overcame many societal problems. Growing up as an African American in an age of discrimination, he had to work twice as hard to get ahead. But Duke Ellington is also known for another reason. He was known for what he gave back to his fellow man. Many performers of that time credited Duke Ellington with the helpful hand and encouragement that contributed to their success.

Duke Ellington once said, "A problem is a chance for you to do your best."

We can look at this quote from two different perspectives. First, we can assume that Duke Ellington was referring to the problems that he faced in life. He was an African American performer in an age when African Americans were not allowed to perform in some of the most important places. The times also made it very difficult to rise to the top of your profession. It was difficult to buy musical instruments and other equipment. Blacks could not travel on the same buses and trains as white performers. They could not stay in the same hotels or eat in the same restaurants. It was very difficult for African

American performers to be able to perform in the South, as simply finding a place to stay or eat was quite difficult.

So, we could simply assume that Duke Ellington was talking about what he had to do in order to be his best. He felt like the problems that he faced gave him a chance to rise to the top. In other words, overcoming problems forced him to work twice as hard. He had to practice his art twice as much. The songs that he wrote had to be twice as good. He had to be twice as persistent as other artists.

That's good advice for us all. But if you read Duke Ellington's statement carefully, it actually has a second meaning. Did you notice that he didn't say who had the problem? We might have assumed that he was referring to one of his own problems. But perhaps he was referring to the problems of others. Think about it. When someone else has a problem, it gives you a chance for you to do your best.

One of the points of the Scout Law is a Scout is helpful. Have you ever seen one of your friends wrestling with a problem and thought to yourself, "Well, if I just stay out of it, he or she will figure out the solution."? But is that what a helpful Scout does?

No. When a helpful Scout sees that one of his or her friends has a problem, they ask their friend if there is anything that you can do to help. There are some problems that your friends just have to work out on their own. And that's okay. If they let you know that they don't need your help, just back off. Be there for them. But respect their wish to handle their problem by themselves. But in many, many situations, your offer of help may be exactly what your friend needs.

Don't always wait until you see that your friend has a problem before you attempt to help them. Surprise your friend with an offer of help even when they don't have a problem! That's what friends are for.

A SCOUT IS HELPFUL #5

GRATITUDE IS A PRESENT THAT YOU GIVE TO OTHERS

One of the most influential inspirational writers was William Arthur Ward. He wrote for numerous publications such as *Reader's Digest.* One of the most impactful things that Mr. Ward said was the following, "Feeling gratitude and not expressing it is like wrapping a present and not giving it."

Have you ever thought about saying something nice to someone or expressing your gratitude to them for something that they have done, only to decide not to say it? But if you had something nice to say to someone, why wouldn't you say it? There are a lot of reasons why someone might "chicken out." They might think that it is not cool to say something nice to a friend. People are always worried about "peer pressure." They might think that someone will think that they are weird if all of a sudden, they come out with something nice. If you think about it and listen to the conversation between two really good friends, it usually consists of them giving playful gibes, needling each other, and giving each other a hard time.

So, people think it might be weird to come out with a kind word or a compliment. But on the other hand, have you ever had someone say to you, "That compliment that you gave me really meant a lot to me."? Remember, your friend is also facing the same "peer pressure" as you are. During the teenage years, people are constantly worried about how they look. Are they wearing the right clothes? Are they doing cool things? Are they interested in the things that everyone else is interested in?

Therefore, when you offer them a compliment or a kind word, it makes them feel good. Research has shown that when you show gratitude to someone else, it also makes you feel good.

Let's go back to the quote from Mr. Ward. If you had spent money on a gift for someone else, wrapped it up, and had it in your hand ready to give to them, would you simply hold onto it and not give the gift to that person? It's possible. Again, those same factors of peer pressure can come into play. At the last moment, you might say to yourself, "I'm not so sure that this is a good gift. What if they don't like it?" But the odds are good that if you go to all the trouble to get the gift, knowing what your friend likes, you're going to give them the gift.

One of the Scout Laws is that a Scout is helpful. Most people think of that as taking some sort of physical action to help other people. Maybe it's helping them with their homework. Maybe it's giving them a ride after school. Maybe it's giving them some tips on their academics or athletics. But one of the most helpful things that you can do is simply give them a kind word, a compliment, or an expression of gratitude.

Next time you have the opportunity, think of that compliment or nice thing as a gift. It's probably the least amount you'll ever pay for something to give to someone else! Don't hang on to the gift. Give it to the friend. It will make them feel better and you feel better.

A SCOUT IS FRIENDLY #1

FIND THE GOOD IN OTHER PEOPLE

Have you ever heard the old statement, "Don't judge a book by its cover."? That statement actually came from an author named George Eliot. But what exactly does that statement mean? Well, every book has a cover. The cover is supposed to show images and have a title that tells the potential reader what the book is about. But that isn't often the case. Have you ever started to read a book that you thought was going to be about one thing, but it turned out to be about something else? Or, did you start to read a book that had a really great cover, but the book did not live up to the cover's greatness? The cover might've been great, but the book was mediocre. So what George Eliot was saying was don't form a conclusion about what the book may be about, simply by what you see on the cover.

If you know anything about the life of George Eliot, it's very ironic that that author made the statement. You see, George Eliot wasn't the author's real name. The author's real name was Mary Ann Evans. He was a she!

You see, back in the Victorian era at the end of the 1800s, many publishers thought that people would not read a book written by a woman. So, they encouraged their female authors to use a name that sounded like a man. And it didn't stop at the end of the Victorian era. One hundred years later, an author named Joanne Rowling submitted to publishers a series of books about a young fellow named Harry Potter. Again, the publishers thought that their audience, made up primarily of young boys, would not want to read a book written by a female. So, they had her change her name to J. K. Rowling.

In the case of these two authors, the cover was people's perception of who the author was. But as George Eliot, or Mary Ann Evans said, "Don't judge the book by the cover."

That advice comes in quite handy as we deal with other people. One of the Scout Laws is that a Scout is friendly. In life, we find that it is easy to be friendly with the most popular people in our class. It's easy to be friendly with the good-looking people. It's easy to be friendly with the best athletes. It's easy to be friendly with the people who have a great personality and a good sense of humor. But those traits are like the cover of the book. Oftentimes, people who aren't the best-looking, or the most talented, or the most athletic, or the most friendly and outstanding can end up being our friend for life. But it requires us to look beyond the obvious external nature of that person. It requires you to make an effort to get to know them, just like you shouldn't form the conclusion about the book until you get to the end of the book.

So, next time you have an opportunity to make a friend, look beyond the obvious exterior of that person. Don't just judge the book by its cover. Get to know them, and you might just make a friend for life.

A SCOUT IS FRIENDLY #2

LIFT UP, DON'T PUT DOWN

The people of the Amish religion are known for their intense devotion to their simple way of life and the friendship they have for each other. One of the things they are most noted for is how they help their neighbors out. If one of the neighbors needs a new barn built, all of the Amish people in that community gather together to build the barn.

There's an old Amish proverb that goes like this, "Instead of putting others in their place, put yourself in their place." We all know what it means to "put someone in their place." In the old days, there were specific places for each person in society. In the old feudal system of the Middle Ages, the poor people were called the serfs. Next, was a class known as the merchants. Next, you had the knights. And finally, you had the upper class, known as the nobility. People were not encouraged to move from one class to another. In fact, the laws and traditions of the time actively discouraged someone from moving up in society. In other words, everyone had their place.

So, if someone tried to move outside of their place in society, it was the role of society to "put them back in their place." While we don't have the strict caste system and levels of society that we used to have, and upward mobility in society is encouraged, people still attempt to put other people in their place.

What this means is if people don't agree with what someone is doing, they take it upon themselves to criticize that person. They may also gossip or talk behind their back.

As the proverb says, we should not attempt to put someone in their place. This means we should not gossip about them, tell lies about them, discourage them, or otherwise provide undue criticism of their efforts to improve themselves. Instead, the proverb encourages us to put ourselves in their place. What does that mean? You may have heard the old Native American proverb of "Never criticize another person until you have walked a mile in their moccasins." The two proverbs have a similar meaning. In both cases, we are told that we should not criticize someone unless we know all of the circumstances. Sure, if you observe someone doing something illegal, unethical, or unduly cruel to someone else, and it is clear what the circumstances are, you should say something to that person. However, we may not know all of the circumstances.

Here's an example. Let's say that you're with one of your friends. They get a call from another friend who wants to borrow something from them. You hear them say no, they can't borrow that item. Your first inclination might be to criticize them for not helping out that friend. But what you may not know is that the other friend had previously borrowed something. They not only didn't return it, but actually destroyed it. Perhaps it's happened more than once. Under those circumstances, it seems more reasonable that your friend is reluctant to loan something to that person until they can learn to be more responsible with those valuable items.

There's yet one more saying that can come into play here. "There are always two sides to the story." This simply means that if we only act on what we observe, we are acting with limited information. Always seek to get the full story and all of the facts before you criticize someone else. In other words, rather than putting that person down, find out their side of the story before you comment on the situation. That's what friends do.

A SCOUT IS FRIENDLY #3

TREAT NEW FRIENDS LIKE OLD FRIENDS

Is everybody familiar with the Muppets? I bet you are. They are some of the most entertaining and educational television characters of all time. The Muppets were created by Jim Henson. Jim Henson was a famous puppeteer. He developed the technology that enabled his puppets to move beyond the sock puppets or puppets on a string called marionettes that had been around for hundreds of years.

The main thing about the Muppets was that they almost became like humans. One of the main characteristics of the Muppets was their friendliness. Oh sure, you had characters like Oscar the Grouch. But at the end of the day, were you still happy to have Oscar come into your living room? Of course.

On the subject of friends, Jim Henson once said, "There's not a word yet for old friends who we've just met." What did he mean by that? Well, we all know what old friends are. They are people we have known for many years. They are people we played with when we were kids. We've gone to school together. We have gone to each other's birthday parties. We've been in Scouts together. We've competed in sports together. Not only has the time that we have known our old friends been lengthy, but our friendship is very close and has grown throughout the years.

But are the only friends we can have those who we have known for many years? If so, others outside our immediate circle of friends are going to see us as being not so friendly! We need to be able to form new friendships. We need to set the goal of making as many new friends as possible.

But the point that Jim Henson was making was that we shouldn't treat our new friends any differently than our old friends. Friends are friends, no matter how long you've known each other. Be open to making new friends. If you spot someone in the cafeteria who is sitting all by themselves, head on over and say hello. Offer to sit down and have lunch with them. Here's the tough thing though. You may have to leave the comfort of your old friends in order to form new friendships.

But I'll bet you if you do head over to sit with someone who apparently has few friends, something interesting will happen. When you go over to meet a new friend, many of your old friends are going to go with you!

One of the Scout Laws is a Scout is friendly. Remember that that doesn't just apply to your current friends. It means that you're going to go out of the way to make new friends. That's what being friendly is all about.

A SCOUT IS FRIENDLY #4

WHAT DO YOU SAY TO OTHER PEOPLE?

Abigail Van Buren was better known as Dear Abby. Amazingly, she and her sister, who wrote the column "Dear Ann Landers," were two of the most famous dispensers of daily advice in the history of newspapers. Dear Abby, as she was known in her column, once said, "The best index to a person's character is how they treat people who can't do them any good, and how they treat people who can't fight back."

Have you ever thought about how you treat other people? You might be thinking, "I treat my friends pretty well. I tried to be respectful of my parents, teachers, and other authority figures. So, I think I treat people pretty well."

But if you think about it, those are the people who it's pretty easy to be nice to. If you are not nice to your friends, they won't be your friends for very long. If you're not nice to your parents, living under the same roof could get to be a challenge. So, it's pretty easy to be nice to those people.

But when the Scout Law says a Scout is friendly, it doesn't have any parentheses after it that say (to your friends and family). No, I'm afraid that when it says a Scout is friendly, it's saying that you should be friendly to all people.

Even if you're not a golfer, you may have heard of the movie *Tin Cup*. In that movie, an unknown golf pro from Texas goes on to challenge the best golfers in the world. His main antagonist is a character named David Simms, played by Don Johnson. When the cameras are on, David Simms is the nicest guy in the world. He's saying nice things about his fellow golfers, he's signing autographs, and he's kissing babies. But when the cameras are turned off, he becomes a whole new person. In the movie, someone asks him for his autograph. He immediately turns on that person, not only refusing to give them an autograph, but questioning why they're even bothering him at all. Unfortunately for him, the love interest in the movie who is trying to choose between Kevin Costner's character, Tin Cup, and David Simms sees a whole new side to David Simms.

Odds are good that you're not thrust in front of the camera on a regular basis. But even if you're not being filmed, other people are watching you. And one of the things that they are watching is how do you treat people around you who were not friends and family. Maybe it's a waitress who's having a hard night at a busy restaurant. Maybe it's your bus driver. Maybe it's the custodian at your school.

How do you treat these people, especially when nobody is watching? Do you acknowledge their existence with a friendly hello or a wave of the hand? Do you ask them how their day is going? Do you compliment them on a job well done? Or do you simply act as if they're not there?

Don't back off on the friendliness that you show for your friends and family. But next time you see someone else, remember that they are someone's friend also. Who knows what's going on in their life at that point in time? They might need a little hug. Be careful because you could get in trouble for that one! But there's no harm in a quick hello, please, or thank you. If you're going to be friendly, be friendly to everyone!

A SCOUT IS FRIENDLY #5

BE NICE, REGARDLESS OF WHAT YOU GET OUT OF IT

If you throw out the question, "Who's the greatest college basketball coach of all time?", you might get a lot of different answers, depending on that person's college loyalty. But in virtually every poll of the experts, the answer is generally John Wooden, the legendary coach of UCLA. After all, he won more college basketball championships than any other college coach.

But not only was Coach Wooden known for winning championships, he was also known for the strong positive effect he had on his players. He took good players and turned them into great players. He turned them into not only winners on the basketball court, but winners in life.

One of the most important bits of advice that Coach Wooden ever gave was, "You have not lived a perfect day until you've done something for somebody who cannot repay you."

It seems like one of the most important things that guides the actions of people is the question, "What's in it for me?" People tend to do things for which they are compensated. It may be financial compensation. It may be the adoration of others. It may be publicity. It may just be the feeling that we got more out of something than we put into it.

One of the points of the Scout Law is that a Scout is friendly. But have you ever found yourself thinking before you do something nice for someone else, "What's in it for me?" Have you ever wondered if you had a choice between doing two nice and friendly things for others, which one would bring you the most benefit?

If you have, then you need to give some more thought to Coach Wooden's advice. While it's nice to receive something back for your actions, that should not be the biggest driving force. The biggest driving force should be the fact that you have done something good for someone else.

If someone can pay for the service from others, such as purchasing a nice house, getting a great job, or getting a fine meal, they may appreciate it. But isn't their level of gratitude much higher when someone gives them something that they couldn't afford? Well, you have in your hands the power to give that very thing. You have the ability to give something to someone that they truly could not afford.

The next time you have the opportunity to do something for someone, don't focus on what's in it for you. Instead, focus on what's in it for them. What can you do to make their day, even if they are totally incapable of repaying you for what you did? You'll both be better off in the end!

A SCOUT IS COURTEOUS #1

TAKE YOUR TIME

How many of you have seen the movie *Willy Wonka & the Chocolate Factory*? It's a really good movie that has a lot of lessons for life. In the movie, Willy Wonka said, "Time is a precious thing. Never waste it."

That's a pretty good lesson for life. Most everything in our lives can be replaced. If we lose money, we can always earn more. If we fail our driver's license test, we can always take it again. But time is the one commodity that, once it is gone, it can never be replaced.

But today, we're going to look at another aspect of time. You have all heard the phrase "take your time." That, of course, means for you to take all the time you need to complete something. But there's another connotation to taking time. And that's taking somebody else's time.

Unless they are a hermit, most everyone likes to talk to other people. They like the companionship. They like the opportunity to tell things about what's going on in their life. They like the ability to communicate important things. But have you ever talked to somebody who talked and talked and talked? Maybe you had something really important that needed to be done. Maybe there was somewhere you needed to be. Or maybe you were just tired of talking about that subject. It's easy for us to recognize when someone else has talked way too much. But it's harder for us to recognize when we've done the same thing to someone else.

One of the Scout Laws is a Scout is courteous. In the age of the internet and social media, some of the common courtesies that we use to have have gone away. Frankly, it's just easier to be rude over the computer than face to face. But courtesy is one thing that hasn't changed for Scouts. It's there in the Law for all to see.

So, one of the ways to show courtesy is to figure out when you are stealing someone else's time. What are some of the ways that you can tell? Well, first of all, look at their body language. Look at the expression on their face. Does their body language say, "Hey, this is really interesting? I'd like to hear more about it." Or does it look like they would really prefer to be somewhere else?

Another thing to look for is are you getting the sense that you're starting to repeat yourself? Here again, watching their body language can be beneficial. Are they starting to nod their head before you even finish your sentence? If so, that's a dead giveaway that you might be saying something that they've already heard.

If you've been talking for a while, and you are starting to repeat the same things, and the body language of the person you're talking to indicates that it's time to move on, then just move on. Stealing someone's time can be as bad as stealing their money or other possessions. Remember, they can never get that time back. So, exercise a little courtesy. Make sure that you respect the other person's precious time.

A SCOUT IS COURTEOUS #2

WATCH WHERE YOU HIT THAT BALL

In 2020, Novak Djokovic, one of the greatest tennis players of all time, was the odds-on favorite to win the U. S. Open Tennis Championships. He really wanted to win that tournament, which is considered one of the top four tennis tournaments in the world. First of all, the grand prize was two million dollars and a neat looking trophy. Second, he trailed Roger Federer for the lead in winning the most Grand Slam tournaments of all time. Federer was nearing the end of his career, and Djokovic was in his prime. So, if he could win the U. S. Open, he would inch closer to the all-time wins total.

Federer was out of the tournament with an injury. The other man with more total wins, Rafael Nadal, was sitting out due to the COVID-19 pandemic. So, Djokovic was the solid favorite to win the tournament.

But after losing a point, in a fit of anger, he hit the ball toward one of the walls. The problem was that there was a line judge standing there. The ball hit the line judge in the head. And the rules say that, if a player hits a line judge with a ball, they are disqualified. He went from winning a major championship and earning two million dollars to being disqualified and paying a large fine.

Although Djokovic hit the ball out of anger, no one thought that he had hit the line judge on purpose. He simply had let his anger overcome him. Despite the fact that he immediately went over to help the judge and apologize profusely, rules are rules. The overwhelming favorite to win the tournament had to be disqualified.

One of the Scout Laws is a Scout is courteous. Does courteous mean not injuring another person? Well, injuring somebody else would definitely not be very courteous. But we don't find ourselves in that position very often. What we do find ourselves in position to do is to make dumb decisions that are fueled by anger, sadness, greed, jealousy, and other emotions. It may be as simple as saying something to someone that hurts their feelings. Like Djokovic, we may not have intended to do it on purpose. Or it may have been something emotional said out of anger. But it was still done.

I'm not saying that we ought to all act like robots. You have emotions. If you bottle them up, it will be even worse. We will all get angry or sad at some point. But when you do, be extra careful that the way that you let those emotions play out does not have a serious negative effect on someone else. Keeping the feelings of other people in mind in all that you say and do is a critical part of being courteous.

A SCOUT IS COURTEOUS #3

CRITICIZE THE ACTIONS, BUT COMPLIMENT THE INDIVIDUALS

Just because someone is among the wealthiest people in the world doesn't always mean that they are a good person. It just means that they are good at making money! But one of the wealthiest people in the world who is generally thought of as being a nice person is Warren Buffett. Warren Buffett is a humble man who not only makes smart financial decisions, but genuinely attempts to be nice to other people.

As the CEO of Berkshire Hathaway, he has a rule that he follows in his dealings with his employees. "Praise by name, criticize by category." If a person in his organization is performing poorly, he doesn't single that person out for blame or humiliation. He criticizes the category or the division of his company that is not performing well. But if an individual makes an outstanding contribution to the company, he singles that person out for praise and thanks. He always builds people up. He never tears them down.

One of the points of the Scout Law is that a Scout is courteous. In our life, we can emulate the management principle given to us by Warren Buffett. Let's look at an example. Let's say that you are on a committee that has been given the task of coming up with a homecoming float. But, for whatever reason, let's say that the float is just not turning out too well. You have three choices. First, you can just go with the flow and turn out a less than commendable product. Trust me, Warren Buffett didn't get to be a successful businessman by turning out unsuccessful products! Your second approach could be to criticize each one of your other committee members. Call them out by name. Embarrass them in front of their peers. Do you think that this approach is going to motivate your fellow workers? Probably not.

Then there is the third approach. Instead of criticizing each person individually, summarize the process itself. You can point out to others some of the issues with your project or product without attacking them individually. But don't just be part of the problem. You may have heard the phrase, "If you're not part of the solution, you're part of the problem." Don't be part of the problem. When you point out areas where the team has fallen short, come in with good solid suggestions for what can be done to improve the process.

Throughout life, you are going to be called upon to work with the team. The courteous way to deal with other people is to not criticize them individually, but rather point out how your team can improve. Not only is it a more courteous approach that will lead to greater teamwork and friendship among the group, but the motivation and direction that it offers will lead to greater success for your team.

A SCOUT IS COURTEOUS #4

ACTIONS SPEAK LOUDER THAN WORDS

One of the most influential thinkers of all time was John Locke. Writing back in the late 1600s, his writings greatly influenced America's founding fathers. Many of his thoughts are presented in the Declaration of Independence and the Constitution. John Locke once wrote, "I have often thought that the actions of men are the best interpreters of their thoughts."

What did he mean by that? Well, have you ever noticed someone who is saying nice things to someone else, but it just doesn't seem to ring true? Maybe it's their nonverbal actions, such as the way that they face the person to whom they are talking. Maybe it's the look in their eyes. They are saying nice things, but their eyes suggest that their statements aren't true. Or maybe it's just the tone of their voice. Maybe it sounds like they are reading from a script, but what they really think is completely different.

That's what John Locke was referring to. You may have heard the phrase, "Walk the walk and talk the talk." Walking the walk is the way that we carry ourselves. How we approach people. How we treat other people. How we follow through on things. Talk the talk refers to what we say to other people.

When somebody tells you to, "Walk the walk and talk the talk," they mean that you should do what you say.

One of the Scout Laws is that a Scout is courteous. So, if we are told to be courteous, does that mean that we simply say nice things to other people? Not if that's not what you truly are thinking. In order to be courteous to someone, you have to go deeper than that. You have to truly want to be nice to them.

Well, I'll be the first to admit that some people make it awfully difficult to be nice to them. But that's what we as Scouts should do. What are some of the things that we can do that enable us to be thinking well of someone in addition to just saying nice things to them? First, if there is something that irritates you about something they do, ask yourself this question: "Is what they do really that important?" Is it something that, with a little effort, you could simply overlook?

Here's another technique. Even the worst person has some good traits. We may have to dig deeply to find them, but they are there! Next time you're dealing with someone whose personality or actions make it difficult for them to be likable, try searching for those traits that are good. Once you find them, focus on them, and not their more dislikable traits.

Don't be the person that John Locke was talking about. The one who thinks one way, but their actions show that they are not in sync. When it comes to being courteous, think it and do it!

A SCOUT IS COURTEOUS #5

BE KIND TO THE EARTH

The Environmental Protection Agency (EPA) was formed to make sure that the environment of our earth was protected. One of the most famous leaders of the EPA was William Ruckelshaus. He once said the following: "Nature provides a free lunch, but only if we control our appetites."

Have you ever known someone who seemed to be always scrounging around for somebody to offer them a free meal? Maybe you've got a friend who always seems to have "alligator arms." After you eat, when the bill arrives, their arms always seem to be too short to reach for the bill.

You probably have also heard the statement that, "There's no such thing as a free lunch." Well, Mr. Ruckelshaus was correct. Nature is one of the few things that does provide to us a free meal. Early in the history of our world, our ancestors survived by eating fruits and berries from the trees. They ultimately learned to plant and harvest vegetables. Their source of meat was the wild animals that they were able to capture and kill. Nowadays, if we are hungry, we can just go hit up the local burger joint. But even processed food is provided by nature.

But in a way, Mr. Ruckelshaus was saying that there's no such thing as a free meal. While nature does offer us sustenance, nature is finite. What does that mean? Finite means that there is a limit to the amount of something. If we keep taking and taking from our planet, eventually it can run out. Not only do we have to limit the amount that we take from nature, but we also have to be willing to put back.

One of the Scout Laws is that a Scout is courteous. We usually think of that in terms of being nice to other people. But there's another area in which we must be courteous. We must be courteous and kind to the planet upon which we live.

Be sensitive to the availability of natural resources. Only take what you need. But also, be willing to give back. Plant a tree. Turn off the lights when you don't need them. Don't use your car when walking is just as easy.

A courteous Scout is kind to other people. But courteous Scouts also realize that nature and its resources are finite. Only take what you need, and be willing to give back when you can.

A SCOUT IS KIND #1

THE WIZARD OF OZ AND THE TIN MAN

Has anyone seen the movie *The Wizard of Oz*? When the movie first came out, it did okay at the box office. But it wasn't considered one of the best movies of all time. But someone had the idea to put it on television and to show it at the same time every year. It began to grow on people and became the classic that it is today.

Do you remember what the Tin Man wanted the Wizard of Oz to give him? He wanted the Wizard to give him a heart. But there is a song by a group named America called "Tin Man." In that song, one of the lines is, "But Oz never did give nothing to the Tin Man that he didn't, didn't already have." In other words, the Tin Man didn't need for the Wizard of Oz to give him a heart. He already had one.

Throughout history, the heart has always been the symbol of emotion. It signifies love. It signifies kindness to others. That is why the heart, or the valentine, is the symbol of love. That's why people say do not break their heart.

In reality, scientists discovered that emotions like love and hatred come from the brain and not the heart. But regardless of whether your kindness to other people comes from the heart or the brain, the important point is that no one can give you kindness. It's something that you already have.

One of the Scout Laws is that a Scout is kind. How do you show kindness to others? One way is to consider the feelings of others before you consider your own. What may be good for you may not necessarily be good for those around you. If someone you know does something good, such as wins an office that they are running for in school, or scores the winning touchdown, or makes an A on the test, how does it make you feel? Do you feel jealous that it wasn't you? Or are you happy for them? Kindness means that you realize that you can both be winners. So, give them a pat on the back or a hearty handshake. That's what kindness is all about.

It's ironic that kindness comes from the brain and not the heart. If you think about it, it was actually the Scarecrow who was asking for the gift of kindness. Because the Scarecrow asked the Wizard for a brain. But as the song could have said, "Oz never did give nothing to the Scarecrow that he didn't, didn't already have." Regardless of whether kindness comes from the heart or the brain, just make sure your kindness comes out!

A SCOUT IS KIND #2

DON'T BE A BACK STABBER

Many years ago, a group called The O'Jays recorded a song called "Back Stabbers". The first line was, "They smile in your face. All the time, they want to take your place. The back stabbers."

Obviously, a back stabber is someone who stabs someone else in the back. Stabbing someone from the front is obviously a terrible thing. But at least the person being stabbed can see the knife coming. They can see who is stabbing them. Stabbing someone from the back has another element to it. The person doing the stabbing is doing it where the victim can't see who is doing the stabbing. There is an element of cowardice involved in stabbing someone in the back. The person doing the stabbing is afraid to even be seen. They operate secretly.

Perhaps one of the most well-known examples of a stabbing comes from history. Have you ever heard of Julius Caesar? Julius Caesar was one of the most famous military leaders. He united all of what is today called Italy into what was then known as the Roman Empire.

But right before he was to be crowned as the Emperor, a group of Roman senators assassinated him by stabbing him to death. History tells us that there were over fifty senators who participated in the stabbing. So, I guess some stabbed him in the back while others stabbed him from other directions. One of the most well-known quotes was allegedly Julius Caesar's last words. Looking up, he saw that one of his assassins was his best friend, Brutus. He said, "Et tu, Brute?" That means, "You too, Brutus?"

I suppose we will never know whether Brutus stabbed Caesar in the back. Probably not, as Caesar was obviously able to see his old friend. But the meaning of his question was quite clear. He felt as if he was being stabbed in the back by his old friend. And that's what a back stabber does.

In life, we don't want you to be a back stabber. The Scout Law tells us that we are to be kind. Stabbing someone in the back is definitely not kind. How do you avoid stabbing your friend in the back? Never betray them. Sure, if your friend does something wrong, you need to confront them about it. If it's bad enough, you may need to go to a teacher, a parent, or some other authority figure. But in your everyday relationship with your friend, don't talk about them behind their back. That's gossip. Don't make up lies about them. Don't tell other people things that they have told you in confidence.

There is another famous saying that is just the opposite of being a back stabber. That saying is, "I've got your back." That means, "I'm right behind you. If anything happens to you, I'm right there with you."

So, let's live a life of kindness. Don't be the back stabber, but the person who has your friend's back.

A SCOUT IS KIND #3

A FULL HOUSE

There is an old Irish proverb that says, "May your home always be too small to hold all your friends."

Have you ever heard the word hospitable? Or hospitality? Hospitality is the act of kindness where you welcome people into your house. There is an industry called the hospitality industry. Many of you may go into it. It refers to people who work in hotels, amusement parks, or other places where tourists go. In all of these examples, whoever is showing hospitality is inviting people to come into their home or place of business.

But did you notice that included in the word hospitality is the word hospital? That's because they both come from the same origin. The origin of both words, hospitality and hospital, is the Latin phrase hospes. It means stranger. You see, that's exactly what a hospital does. It is a place that takes in people who it doesn't know and ministers to their medical needs.

Well, that's a part of hospitality. In the old days, it referred to taking in strangers. You might remember the parable of the Good Samaritan. Did the Good Samaritan know the person he encountered who had been robbed and beaten on the road from Jerusalem to Jericho? No, he was a perfect stranger. And yet, the traveler rescued the other traveler, tended to his wounds, took him into the nearest town, and left money to pay for his medical treatment. He did all of this for a stranger. And that's where the word hospitality comes from.

I'm afraid that nowadays, you have to be careful about taking strangers into your home. As you grew up, your parents cautioned you to be careful around strangers. It's a sad fact, but there are many people out there with the intention of doing harm. So, while we aren't able to welcome strangers into our homes like people may have done in the old days, we can still show hospitality.

The Scout Law tells us that a Scout is kind. What are some ways that you might show kindness to others through your hospitality? Well, is there someone in your school cafeteria who is shunned by others because they might be shy or a little different? If so, show kindness! Go over and introduce yourself. Offer to sit with them at lunch.

When it comes to sports at your school, is there someone who just isn't the best athlete in the world? Are they commonly embarrassed because they never get chosen for the team? Well, if you're picking up sides, and you have the chance, go ahead and pick them for your team. You may not win the game, but the kindness that you've shown to others will go much further than simply winning or losing a game.

If you've made a new friend in your troop, school, or church, invite them over to your house. Make sure to tell your parents first. They don't need surprises! But kindness is all about showing friendship to strangers, as well as those you know.

A SCOUT IS KIND #4

THE GREATEST ACT OF KINDNESS

An anthropologist is a scientist who looks back in time to study the history of mankind and how people have changed over time. They're the ones that you see out in the desert, sifting through the sand, looking for evidence of how previous humans led their daily lives.

There are two different definitions of civilization. One definition refers to the different and multiple civilizations that have existed over time. For example, you have the Greeks, the Babylonians, the Persians, and the Egyptians. These are all examples of different civilizations that rose and fell over the years.

But there is another definition of civilization. That refers to when humans became civilized. In other words, when did they move from a very simple life of simply trying to exist from one day to the next, to begin doing things such as learning to farm? Or when did they develop language where they could communicate with each other? Or when did they begin to write things down so that they could share information and ideas and pass stories on to future generations. These things are associated by anthropologists with becoming more civilized.

Years ago, anthropologist Margaret Mead was asked what she considered to be the first sign of civilization. Everyone expected her to say the invention of tools or the use of fire. But she said the first sign of civilization that she saw was a human bone that had been broken and then healed. She said that with animals, a broken bone meant you were destined to die. Even in our modern times, if a million-dollar racehorse breaks a leg, it is put to death. Why? In ancient times, a broken leg meant that a human couldn't run from a threat. They couldn't hunt or fish. They were easy prey for beasts. But the healed bone meant someone had taken in this person, tended to their wound, and protected and nourished them until they were able to recover. Helping someone through difficulty is where civilization starts.

What Dr. Mead was saying is that when mankind developed kindness, that was when they became civilized. Kindness is the act of placing the needs of someone else above our own needs. For example, if you gave up your seat on a crowded bus to an elderly person, you've shown kindness. But what you've done is given up your need for comfort in favor of someone who needs that seat more than you do. As a young person, your time is precious. You want to spend every spare moment that you have having fun. But we read stories about young people who spend their extra time raising money to buy blankets, shampoo, and so on for homeless people. They are placing the needs of those homeless people ahead of their own need for time and money. This, simply, is the act of kindness.

As a Scout, we are told to be kind to others. This may not be as extreme as mending the broken bone of your best friend so that they can recuperate and outrun animals! But during our average day, there are countless examples of how we can place the needs of others ahead of our own. The next time you have a chance to do a favor for someone else and place their needs ahead of your own, take that as an opportunity to show kindness. Just do it!

A SCOUT IS KIND #5

DON'T ALWAYS ASSUME YOU KNOW ALL OF THE FACTS

Robin Williams was considered to be one of the funniest actors and comedians of all time. Millions of people were entertained by his funny comedy sketches, television programs, and movies. But underneath the surface, Robin Williams was fighting many demons. He ended up taking his own life. Perhaps in a foreshadowing of what was going on in his own life, Robin Williams once said, "Everyone you meet is fighting a battle you know nothing about. Be kind. Always."

It's easy to be critical of other people. We might see them doing something that we wouldn't do. Or doing something that we've been taught is wrong. But before you jump to a conclusion, the kind thing to do is to make sure you have all of the facts.

There is a story that was making its way around the internet many years ago. I don't know if it's true or not, but it has enough elements that I believe it could be true. Either way, it can teach us a valuable lesson. A young father got onto a bus with his four children. The other riders of the bus noticed that the children were acting up. You can even use the words out of control. Rather than attempt to discipline his children, the young father just sat there as if in a daze. Finally, after this went on for some time, an elderly woman approached the young man. She began to berate him for his poor parenting skills. She pointed out what a distraction his children's behavior was to the rest of the people on the bus. Over and over again, she scolded him for not properly disciplining his children.

Curiously, instead of looking up at the woman, the father continued to stare at the floor of the bus. Finally, after the elderly woman seemed to run out of words, the young father looked up with tears in his eyes. He said, "I'm very sorry about the behavior of my children. You see, their mother just died a few days ago. We're just coming from the funeral. So, I'm afraid my children are a little emotional. And I'm afraid I'm a bit distracted."

The elderly woman immediately became silent as she understood the magnitude of the situation. And instead of berating the father for his lack of parenting skills, she immediately offered to help him watch the kids while he mourned the loss of his wife.

Obviously, you will encounter situations where you need to say or do something immediately. If someone is doing something dangerous that is putting their life or the life of others in jeopardy, you don't always have time to ask a lot of probing questions. You simply have to take action. But most of the time that we judge the behavior of others, we do have time to find out more about the situation. The Scout Law tells us that a Scout is to be kind. Oftentimes, kindness comes not from pointing out someone's flaws, but comes from finding out more about what has contributed to the flaws and offering to help that person resolve that situation. There's a lot of wisdom to the old saying, "Look before you leap."

A SCOUT IS OBEDIENT #1

TAKE AUSTRIA

Historians can argue over who was the greatest military commander of all time. Arguments can be made that it is Alexander the Great, or Julius Caesar, or Genghis Khan. But there is no argument among historians that among the list of the world's greatest military commanders, Napoleon Bonaparte would have to be in the top group.

As the Emperor of France, Napoleon set out to conquer the world. But conquering the world is not an easy thing to do! Napoleon quickly learned that he could not be in all places at all times. So, he had to delegate his command of the French army to other generals within his army. But that didn't always go as well as Napoleon would have liked.

While Napoleon was fighting in Spain, he realized that a threat to his country of France was coming from the country of Austria. He delegated one of his generals to march toward Austria. His instructions were crystal clear. The general was to move into Austria and attacked Austria before Austria could attack France, realizing that the best defense was a good offense. Napoleon ordered his general to attack Austria.

However, after many weeks, he realized that his general had not obeyed his orders. For whatever reason, the general had proceeded to the Austrian border, but hadn't moved into

Austria and engaged the Austrian army. Finding a lull in his war in Spain, Napoleon rushed to the Austrian border. His statement to his general was simple, but carried much meaning. What he said was, "If you are going to take Austria, take Austria."

This advice applies to us today. Oftentimes, we are instructed to do things that we may not want to do. The instructions may come from our parents, from a teacher, from a policeman, from a coach, or from any other person of authority. But even though we may not want to do what we are instructed to do, that is what obedience is all about.

Now let me be very clear about this. In life, you will find people in authority who order you to do something that isn't right. It may be illegal. It may be unethical. It may be far too dangerous for the situation. In very limited circumstances, you may find that it is not right for you to comply with that order. In that case, the best thing that you can do is to find another similar person of authority, and appeal to them to intervene in the situation.

But that's not what I'm talking about. I'm talking about orders that are given to you that need to be done. For example, your parents may ask you to clean your room. That's something that you need to do as part of a household that works together as a family. There may be many reasons why you don't want to do it. You may be tired. You may want to play with your friends instead. Or you just might like a messy room! But being obedient to your parents, teachers, and other people of authority is what obedience is all about.

So next time your parents ask you to clean your room, remember the quote from Napoleon. And if you're going to clean your room, clean your room.

A SCOUT IS OBEDIENT #2

JUST BE YOURSELF

One of the Scout Laws is to be obedient. Many people think that obedience only applies to your relationship with somebody else. In other words, obedient means that you are obeying someone of authority. It could be your parents. It could be a teacher. It could be one of your Scout leaders or a law enforcement officer. But they assume that obedience only applies to obeying someone else. But is that always the case?

One of the greatest writers of all time was the Irish writer Oscar Wilde. He once said, "Be yourself; everyone else is already taken."

You have all probably heard of the advice to be yourself. Be yourself means to try not to act like someone else who you are not. Why would someone want to act like someone else? Well, we might think that we are not as "cool" as someone else. Or we are not as good-looking as someone else. Or we may think that they are smarter than we are. So, what we try to do is to act like them. We figure that if they are successful in life, if we act like them, we will also be successful. So, we try to dress like them, talk like them, walk like than, and even think like them.

What's the matter with that? The problem is that, as much as we try to be someone else, we can never succeed at that. Why? Because we are ourselves. We can't be someone else. Or as Oscar Wilde said, they are already taken. When people see that we are trying to be someone else, we come off looking like a phony. People don't like phonies. They like people they can trust. If they can't even trust you to be true to yourself, how can they trust you to be true to them?

So, what does this have to do with obedience? Well, who you are has been, in large part, dictated to you since your birth. Your genes and chromosomes determine what color hair you will have, what color skin you will have, and what color eyes you will have. Your genetic makeup can determine what diseases you might be susceptible to. There's an old argument called nature versus nurture. The nature side argues that most of who we are comes from that genetic makeup. The nurture side argues that much of who we are is determined by how we are nurtured by our parents, how we are raised, what type of things we experience, how we are educated, and so forth. But regardless of how much of who we are comes from the way we are wired, and how much comes from the way we are raised, the point is that we still are who we are. And it's important to obey who we are.

If we try to disobey who we are, it's just like disobeying anyone else of authority. In other words, one of the most important authorities in your life is yourself! So, the next time you attempt to be someone else, remember, they are already taken! Be true to yourself. Obey yourself. And remember the Scout Law that says that we are to be obedient.

A SCOUT IS OBEDIENT #3

PRACTICE, PRACTICE, PRACTICE

There is an old saying that is attributed to an anonymous source. That means that nobody knows who said it. But it's a good saying for life. It goes like this: "How do you get to Carnegie Hall? Practice, practice, practice."

If you don't know what Carnegie Hall is, the saying doesn't make much sense. Carnegie Hall is a performing arts theater in New York City. It's where some of the most talented people in the world perform. Very few people will ever get to perform at Carnegie Hall.

The joke is that someone is simply asking for directions to Carnegie Hall. But the way they asked the question, "How do you get to Carnegie Hall?" could be interpreted as asking what you have to do to be able to perform at Carnegie Hall. So, the answer to the question is, "practice, practice, practice."

Years ago, a book came out by author Malcolm Gladwell. In that book, he made the claim that, based on his research, to become really good at anything, a person had to perform that task or action for ten thousand hours. So, if a violinist wanted to get good enough to perform at Carnegie Hall, they had to practice a minimum of ten thousand hours. Whether or not ten thousand is the right number of hours, it sure is true that in order for someone to become a concert violinist, they need to practice, practice, practice.

One of the Scout Laws is that a Scout is obedient. But what does obedience have to do with practicing a skill? Well, when we normally think of obedience, we normally think of it as obeying someone in authority. Or we might think of it as obeying a rule, such as a speed limit.

But there's another aspect to obedience. When we are told to be obedient, it can also mean that we should be obedient to the goals and objectives that we have set for ourselves. Let's say that we wanted to lose weight. We set out a plan for diet and exercise. But when it comes time to choose between a hot dog and a salad, temptation sets in and the rule that we set for ourselves goes out the door. Or when we know that we should be walking around the block, but playing another video game seems like a better idea.

When you choose to play another video game instead of doing something that you set as a goal for yourself, are you obeying your own wishes? Definitely not.

None of us are probably going to get the chance to perform at Carnegie Hall. But we are all going to have the opportunity to set goals and objectives to better our lives. Be obedient to those goals that you have set. Resist the temptations to be lazy and fall short of your goals. Instead of practice, practice, practice, our obedience to ourselves can be to do it, do it, and do it.

A SCOUT IS OBEDIENT #4

OBEY YOUR OWN DESIRE TO ACHIEVE

Back in 1928, an author named John Augustus Shedd wrote a book called *Salt from My Attic.* It was full of inspirational thoughts. But the quotation that John Augustus Shedd is best known for was, "A ship in harbor is safe, but that's not what ships are for."

Everybody has their own little safe zone. For a ship, it's usually the harbor. There, they are safe from the winds and waves of the ocean. They have access to food and supplies. They can go into dry dock and get repairs. But the point that Mr. Shedd was making is that sitting in a dock is not what that ship is for. The ship is designed to sail to faraway places. It's designed to help other people by delivering valuable supplies. It takes people to their ultimate destinations.

So, the ship could stay in its safe zone. But it is totally useless. It is not achieving the mission that it was designed for. The same could be said for us. Are we taking the route of safety and security? Or are we stepping out and achieving the mission for which we were designed?

One of the Scout Laws is a Scout is obedient. We normally think that simply means that a Scout should obey people of authority. But if you think about it, there's another meaning of obedience. Obedience means doing what we are told. But in many ways, life tells us what to do. Our own self tells us what to do. For example, let's say you enjoy athletics. Maybe you're even pretty good at it. But you're worried about whether you can do what athletes need to do. Maybe you're worried about being embarrassed when you fail. Maybe you're worried about being hurt. In this case, the safe course of action would be to simply sit out and not participate in sports. But is that what you and your life are telling you to do?

The same could be said for academics, school politics, leadership, even joining a scout troop. In life, you need to follow your heart. Sure, if your heart is telling you to do something that you shouldn't do, remember, there is another Scout Law that says a Scout is clean. The Scout Oath tells us to be morally straight. So, that's not the obedience that I'm talking about. But if you have a desire to do something that will build you up and benefit society, don't be like the ship that sits safely in the harbor. Be the ship that takes chances and sets out on its mission.

A SCOUT IS OBEDIENT #5

LEARN TO OBEY YOUR OWN RULES

One of the most common questions that I get from Scouts is, "How do I say no to the people who want me to do something that is wrong?" It's a great question. With all of the peer pressure that you experience, it's difficult to say no to your friends and family when they tell you that you should do something that you know that you shouldn't. Nobody wants to look like a coward. Everybody wants to be part of the group. So, it's tough to just say no. But here's some great advice that I once heard.

Steve Kamb, the founder of NerdFitness.com, once said that the best and most polite excuse is just to say you have a rule. "I have a rule that I don't decide on the phone." "I have a rule that I don't accept gifts." "I have a rule that I don't speak for free anymore." "I have a rule that I am home for bath time with the kids every night." People respect rules, and they accept that it's not you rejecting the offer, request, demand, or opportunity, but the rule allows you no choice. So, you might want to give that technique a try.

But there is a funny thing about rules. If we set a rule for ourselves, we have to obey it! One of the Scout Laws is that a Scout is obedient. We usually think of that in the context of being obedient to our parents, teachers, or other figures of authority. But there is another aspect to obedience. We have to obey our own rules.

Let's say that someone asked you to borrow a large sum of money. You have an inkling as to what they want to use the money for. And it's not a good thing. You really don't want to be part of financing whatever activity they want the money for. But they try every trick in the book. They play on your friendship. They play on your loyalty. The temptation is to give in and give them the money. But then you remember the advice from Mr. Kamb. And you say, "My rule is that I do not give large loans to other people without talking to my parents first." It's a rule. It has to be followed. End of discussion.

But then, the next day, another friend asks you for a large loan that you know is going to a good cause. It's the type of thing that you want to support. You want to be helpful for your friend. But remember your rule? If you give a loan to the second friend without checking with your parents, and your first friend becomes aware of it, what kind of credibility have you established?

So, wisely figure out a way to create good rules for you to follow. But then, be faithful to obey those rules. It may sound complicated, but life always gets easier when you make good rules for yourself and then follow them.

A SCOUT IS CHEERFUL #1

IT'S HOW YOU DO IT

The two greatest professional golfers in history are generally considered to be Jack Nicklaus and Tiger Woods. A strong argument could be made that Jack Nicklaus is the greatest golfer of all time. After all, he won more major golf tournaments than any other person.

Jack Nicklaus created his own golf tournament, held at one of the courses that he designed. One year, Jack Nicklaus was sitting in the television booth being interviewed by the sportscasters. While he was in the booth, a golfer hit a ball that came to rest at a fence right on the out of bounds line.

When the golfer arrived at his ball, it was on the other side of the out of bounds fence. But he felt like enough of the ball was in bounds that he should not be assessed a one-stroke penalty. He called over to the rules official. That's the golf equivalent of a referee or an umpire. The rules official looked at the location of the ball and declared that the ball was out of bounds. The player rudely told the rules official that he wanted a second opinion. Sure enough, when a higher-ranking rules official came over and looked at the ball, he also declared that the ball was out of bounds. Instead of thanking the official, the golfer rudely stomped away.

Up in the booth, Jack Nicklaus witnessed the exchange on the television monitor. When the commentator asked Mr. Nicklaus what he thought, Mr. Nicklaus replied, "He is perfectly within the rules to ask for a second ruling, but..." Jack Nicklaus' comment of "but" hung in the air. It said a lot about what he thought of the golfer's actions.

As a stickler for the rules, Jack Nicklaus knew that, indeed, the golfer was well within his rights to ask for a second opinion. But that wasn't what Mr. Nicklaus noted.

You see, sometimes it's not what you do, but how you do it that is important. One of the points of the Scout Law is that a Scout is cheerful. In life, like this golfer, we will be placed in positions that are not a lot of fun. But how we handle these situations is what determines whether that Scout has been cheerful.

This golfer could have thanked the first rules official for taking the time to come over and assess the situation and said something like, "Thank you for the ruling. But would it be possible for me to see if the rules supervisor sees the situation differently?" But he didn't. He was rude in the way that he treated the first rules official. To compound the problem, he was rude to the second rules official. Instead of simply thanking the rules official for giving him the second ruling, he chose to simply storm away.

As a Scout, you will be more closely observed than the average person. People know that you are supposed to be cheerful and kind. They will observe you closely and just hope that you do something rude or stupid that they can catch on video and upload to the internet. Don't give them the chance.

A SCOUT IS CHEERFUL #2

YOU GOTTA BE YOU

One of the most popular singers of all time was Sammy Davis, Jr. As an African American, he broke all kinds of color barriers when he began singing back in the 1930s. One of his most famous songs was "I've Gotta Be Me." Here is one of the stanzas:

"Whether I'm right or whether I'm wrong. Whether I find a place in this world or never belong. I gotta be me, I've gotta be me!"

What does it mean when we say that we've got to be me? Or you may have heard it expressed as you've got to be yourself. Simply put, it means that you shouldn't try to be someone other than who you really are. Some people go through life trying to pretend that they are someone other than who they are. They try to act like they are richer than they are. Or that they are smarter than they are. Or that they are better looking than they are. So, what's the matter with that?

I think it's important to differentiate between trying to be the best that you can be and trying to be something that you aren't. There's nothing wrong with studying hard in order to get smarter. In fact, we should all do that. There's nothing wrong with using good hygiene to try to make yourself look as good as possible. There's nothing wrong with working hard to place yourself in a better financial position.

But what I'm talking about is when you don't achieve those things, but rather you simply pretend like you do. There are several problems with pretending like you are somebody that you are not. In the first place, it's a lie. I always wondered why "honest" wasn't one of the Scout Laws. But the Scout Oath says, "On my honor," so I suppose that's close enough! The bottom line is that we are to be honest. Living a life that's a lie doesn't meet that standard.

Second, psychiatrists would tell you that pretending that you are someone other than who you really are can lead to all kinds of significant psychological problems and mental illness. And there's yet one more reason. People can tell when someone isn't being themselves. And that leads to a lack of trust. So, be yourself.

However, I'm going to throw one more thing at you. One of the Scout Laws is that a Scout is cheerful. If your natural inclination is to always be gloomy, in a bad mood, or pessimistic, people are not going to want to be around you. It doesn't take much extra work to look on the positive side of things.

So, feel free to be yourself. But always strive to be your most cheerful self.

A SCOUT IS CHEERFUL #3

SPREAD THE LIGHT

Edith Wharton was one of the most famous American novelists of all times. She is best known for becoming the first female author ever to win the prestigious Pulitzer Prize for Literature for her novel *The Age of Innocence.*

Ms. Wharton once said, "There are two ways of spreading light: to be the candle or the mirror that reflects it."

Unfortunately, darkness has gotten kind of a bad rap. Lots of good things take place in darkness. For example, we wouldn't be able to see the beautiful stars in the sky if it wasn't for darkness. Getting a good night's sleep is always easier in the dark! Can you imagine what it would be like to see a fireworks display in broad daylight?

But bringing light to the darkness doesn't always have to do with literal sunlight versus the dark of night. It often takes a moral perspective.

Bringing light into the darkness has always been seen as a symbol of bringing goodness to something bad. It stands for education. It symbolizes moral values. So, from a morality perspective, bringing light to darkness has always been seen as a good thing.

In addition, one of the strongest symbolisms of bringing light to darkness has to do with being cheerful. Have you ever heard the statement, "He or she lit up the room."?

One of the Scout Laws is that we are to be cheerful. I think that the quote from Ms. Wharton demonstrates to us two ways that we can be cheerful. First, we can be the candle. In other words, we can be the source of the cheerful light that brings good cheer to everyone around us.

But her second example, while subtle, is equally as effective. What happens when you shine light into a mirror? The mirror reflects the light out to a broad area. We can also be like that mirror. You may not feel that your personality is such that you are the one who lights up the room. You may feel a little more introverted than extroverted. But that's okay. Your role in life may be to take the cheerfulness and exuberance shown by other people and reflect those back over the group.

Do you know someone who is really grumpy? When someone says something exciting, their personality seems to dampen that excitement. And what is the general reaction to their negativity? Well, it sure isn't positivity. Don't be like that grump. Take the excitement of others and reflect that excitement and cheerfulness out over everyone that you can. Even if you can't be the candle, you can still be the mirror!

A SCOUT IS CHEERFUL #4

DON'T BE AFRAID TO LAUGH AT YOURSELF

One of the early pioneers of comedy on television and in the movies was Carl Reiner. Starting out as a comedy writer, he soon had his own television program. He directed numerous movies that set the standard for comedy.

Mr. Reiner once said, "Inviting people to laugh at you while you are laughing at yourself is a good thing to do. You may be the fool, but you are the fool in charge."

Have you ever seen people who just can't stand it when other people laugh at them? These people have to feel like they are constantly in charge. The worst thing that could happen to them would be that someone perceives that they made a mistake. If an embarrassing video of them ever appeared on the internet, they would spend all of their time trying to figure out how to get it taken down instead of enjoying a good laugh with everyone else.

But everyone makes mistakes. One of the greatest skills that someone can have is the ability to make a mistake and laugh with others at the mistake that they have made. The ability to laugh at yourself shows humility. It shows that you don't consider yourself to be mistake-free and better than others. But, rather, it shows that you are just one of the gang.

But Mr. Reiner takes that even further. He says that we should actually invite people to laugh at us while we're laughing at ourselves. Think about the jesters back in the courts of the kings and queens. Their job was to make everyone laugh. And what were they called? They were called the fool. But think about it for a moment. In fact, the fools were actually controlling the situation. They were determining who everyone was watching. They were determining what people were enjoying. Their ability to command the attention of others began with their ability to laugh at themselves and to encourage others to laugh at them.

One of the Scout Laws is a Scout is cheerful. Grumpy people who cannot laugh at themselves or get upset when others laugh at them are definitely not considered cheerful. Don't take life so seriously. If you make a mistake, give it a good laugh. Laugh along with others as they enjoy the situation. You will definitely be considered more cheerful, and life will definitely be more fun.

A SCOUT IS CHEERFUL #5

MAKE UP YOUR MIND TO BE HAPPY

One of the most famous American writers was Edith Wharton. In an era where women writers weren't exactly encouraged, Edith Wharton wrote groundbreaking novels, including *The Age of Innocence* and *Ethan Frome*.

Ms. Wharton once said, "If you make up your mind not to be happy, there's no reason why you shouldn't have a fairly good time."

Think about that for a second. Throughout life, you come up with goals. They may be as simple as which fast food restaurant to hit up for your next meal. Maybe it's something really complex, like getting through the final exam without embarrassing yourself!

Or your goal setting may be more long term and complex, such as deciding which college you want to go to. Or deciding what occupation you want to have. Or where you want to live? Should you get an apartment or should your goal be to save enough money to buy a house? But regardless of what it is, all throughout life, we set goals for ourselves.

You may not think about it this way, but one of the goals that you set is either to be happy or to be miserable. Now you may be thinking, "Wait a minute. I don't choose to be miserable. It just seems to happen to me." Well, of course, bad things happen to people through no effort of their own. Bad things can happen to good people. But there are many cases where people seem to bring unhappiness upon themselves. We call them pessimists. You may have heard the analogy about the glass that's holding half of the water that it can hold. Optimists see the glass as half full. Pessimists see the glass as half empty.

So, when it comes to our attitude about life, we can definitely set our own goals. If we set the bar low, as Ms. Wharton suggests, it's pretty easy to achieve our objective. But will we be happy that we achieved our goal? No, because our goal was not to be happy!

One of the Scout Laws is a Scout is cheerful. Therefore, we know which direction we are supposed to go. Next time you set goals for yourself, be they short-term goals or long-term goals, make sure that being happy and cheerful is one of your objectives. If you achieve the goal, you'll be happy that you made it, but you will also be happy in life!

A SCOUT IS THRIFTY #1

KEEP TRACK OF YOUR MONEY

There's an old joke that is told. Two parents set up their child with a checking account before he or she headed off to college. After a couple of weeks, they got a call from their bank. They were told that their child had overdrawn their checking account. They called up their child at college and asked how they could have overdrawn the checking account. The student responded, "How could I be overdrawn with my checking account? I still have checks left."

Don't laugh. We've all done something similar. We've all lost track of how much money we have in our pocket, in the bank, underneath the mattress of our bed, or buried in mayonnaise jars in the backyard. It's easy to do.

But one of the Scout Laws is that a Scout is thrifty. Thrifty doesn't just have to mean stingy. You don't have to be Ebenezer Scrooge in the first part of *A Christmas Carol* in order to be considered thrifty. No, thrifty means that you simply do a good job managing your financial assets.

What does that include? Well, it starts with keeping track of how much money you have. But it goes beyond that. It also includes knowing what your sources of income are. Do you have a part-time job? Do you mow lawns? Do you babysit? Do you get an allowance from your parents? All of these are sources of income. Knowing how much money you have isn't enough. Your financial situation can change immediately as more income flows in.

But the next part of the equation is knowing what your expenses are. Have you ever done the exercise where you actually keep track of all of your expenses? Going to a movie may not seem like it's a big expense. Until you add up the cost of the ticket, the popcorn, the soft drink, the candy, etc. Buying an occasional drink at the convenience store may not seem like a big expense. But if you add up all of those purchases over the course of a month, most people are shocked to see how much money they spent.

So, part of being thrifty is good financial management. Always strive to know how much money and other assets you have. Have a good feel for what your income is. Have a good feel for what your expenses are. And, bottom line, make sure the amount of money going out the door doesn't exceed the amount coming in the door!

A SCOUT IS THRIFTY #2

GROSS HABITS AND NET INCOME

One of the most dashing Hollywood actors of all time was Errol Flynn. He was known for his swashbuckling movies, such as *The Adventures of Robin Hood.* But like many Hollywood celebrities, he had a problem. He liked to spend money. He had a very addictive personality. His bad habits not only got him into trouble, but wasted away the fortune that he made as an actor. Of course, he attempted to blame it on others. It was the fault of his agent. It was the fault of his manager. It was the fault of his accountant. But in the end, it was his fault.

At least at one point, he seemed to acknowledge the problem. He said, "My problem lies in reconciling my gross habits with my net income."

In accounting, you have two very important terms, gross and net. Gross income is the total amount of income that we have coming in. The word "gross" has taken on a different meaning in our society. It's taken on a negative connotation. If we call something gross, it's not exactly a compliment. But the original term was very positive. Gross income is the total amount of funds that you have coming in.

But from your gross income you have to subtract your expenses. Once your expenses are subtracted, you're left with what is called your net income. Net income is actually more important than gross income. Errol Flynn learned the hard way that it didn't really matter how much gross income he had coming in. Because, with his wild spending habits, net income, or the amount that he had left over, was very small. And what contributed to his high expenses? As he put it, it was his gross habits.

One of the Scout Laws is that a Scout is thrifty. You don't necessarily have to spend your entire life focusing on increasing your gross income. You've probably heard the statement from Scripture that, "The pursuit of money is the root of all evil." Note that the statement doesn't say that money is the root of all evil. We need money to survive. It drives our commercial system. Things in life are not free. We need money in order to trade for goods and services. No, it's the pursuit of money that is the root of all evil. Don't focus your entire life on simply accumulating as much money as possible.

But once your level of income is determined, it's your expenses that you should seek to control. As a thrifty Scout, closely monitor your expenses. Make sure that your gross habits don't get out of control. And if you follow that simple formula, you'll end up with a reasonable net income that will make your life comfortable.

A SCOUT IS THRIFTY #3

WORK HARD TO MAKE THINGS BETTER

One of the most famous German playwrights was Bertolt Brecht. He once said, "Just because things are the way they are, doesn't mean they stay that way."

That advice could apply to a lot of areas of our life. But I would like to look at that advice in the context of a particular area of our life. One of the Scout Laws is that a Scout is thrifty. When we generally think of thrifty, we think that we should be careful in our spending, making sure that we do not spend more than we have coming in as income. We might also think of thrifty in terms of putting away savings for the future.

Being a thrifty Scout does include all of that. But there is another aspect of thriftiness. I believe that when the Scout Law says that a Scout is to be thrifty, it takes in a lot more aspects of our personal finances. Let's look at one particular example. In analyzing poverty, experts find that poverty is caused by many different things. Poverty may be caused because society has a high unemployment rate. There simply aren't enough jobs for everyone. Poverty can also be due to extreme circumstances. For example, a major medical issue could rob a family of their savings.

But experts have found that the number one source of poverty is what is called generational poverty. People have grown up in poverty. Their parents were poor. Their grandparents before them were poor. Unfortunately, people in that situation simply feel like poverty is the norm for their life. These are the cards that they have been dealt.

That's when the quote from Mr. Brecht comes in. Just because things are the way they are doesn't mean they stay that way. Just because you or your family have been dealt a certain set of cards doesn't mean that you can't discard them and get some different cards. Take a look at your financial situation. It doesn't have to be extreme poverty. It could simply be that the bill to fix your car is more than you have in the bank. It could be that you got laid off from your job. Whatever the negative situation is, don't just assume that that's the way things have to be.

Sit down and honestly assess the situation. Is there another job out there that you can get? It may take some work to find it. But don't just assume that you were not meant to have a good job. Are there some expenses that you can cut?

There are a lot of aspects of being thrifty. But one of the most important is to never assume that the current situation must remain a permanent situation. If you find yourself in a difficult financial situation, sit down and intelligently assess the situation. Seek good financial advice. Don't just throw in the towel and assume that things can't get better. Then, do what it takes to turn around that financial situation for the good of you and your family.

A SCOUT IS THRIFTY #4

THINGS CAN GET WORSE IF YOU DON'T MAKE THEM BETTER

There is a British lawmaker named Damian Green. Apparently, he is a pretty pessimistic sort of guy. He once made the statement, "There's no situation so bad that it can't get worse tomorrow."

While that's a pretty pessimistic statement, unfortunately it can be true. Oftentimes, our reaction to a bad situation is to simply do nothing. You may have heard the term, "analysis paralysis." That happens when someone thinks that the best way to get out of a difficult situation is to analyze it. And analyze it. And analyze it some more. The problem is they simply keep analyzing it over and over again, and never take action to correct the situation.

You're probably familiar with the firing sequence of, "ready, aim, fire." But with analysis paralysis, instead of ready, aim, fire, our firing sequence becomes, "ready, aim, aim, aim…" We simply are so paralyzed that we are incapable of taking action to remedy the situation.

One of the Scout Laws is that a Scout is thrifty. If you think about it, one of the areas in life where we are most likely to encounter a negative situation is in the area of finances. Sure, we might get jilted by that special someone with whom we wanted to go to the prom. Yes, we might not get the job for which we applied. We most likely will suffer a flat tire or some other automotive issue. But all of those situations are easily remedied. The next day, the problem doesn't seem to be quite as big as it was the day before.

But when it comes to finances, issues become more severe. We have income which is derived from our work salaries, allowances, interest on our savings, etc. We have expenses that come from our basic needs, but also our hobbies and other indulgences. If we find ourselves in a situation where the expenses are larger than the income, we have a real problem.

And this is a classic case where Mr. Green's pessimistic statement kicks in. If we don't take action to either increase our income or to decrease our expenses, our economic situation will only get worse and worse. And a negative financial situation impacts more than just our wallet. It can cause sleepless nights. It can sap our energy. It can take away our appetite. It can affect our relationship with our friends and family.

A thrifty Scout realizes that if we have a negative financial situation, analyzing it to death isn't going to help. Choosing to avoid it isn't going to help either. No, they recognize that the best solution is to go on the offensive. Quickly, figure out what the problem is, get good sound financial advice from people you trust, and take action to fix the situation as rapidly as possible.

A SCOUT IS THRIFTY #5

ALWAYS DO THINGS THE RIGHT WAY

I'm sure that you are all familiar with the Navy SEALs. The Navy SEALs are one of the most elite fighting forces in the world. Their selection process is rigorous. Only the best are allowed to join. Their training is some of the most difficult in the world. The principles that they follow can mean the difference between life and death.

We could all learn from some of the principles of the Navy SEALs. One of their principles is the following: "There are two ways to do something: The right way, and again."

Another way to say this is the common piece of advice, "If you don't have time to do it right the first time, when are you going to find time to fix it?" There are many reasons why we should do things right the first time. When it comes to morals, we should follow the Scout Oath, which tells us to be morally straight. Or the Scout Law that tells us that a Scout is clean. We should always strive to do the right thing when it comes to dealing with other people, representing ourselves in front of others, and simply living life as a good person.

But doing the right thing also has more everyday functions. Doing the right thing means to analyze the situation and then make the best decision. For example, let's say that you are building something. You may have heard the old saying related to drilling a hole: "Measure twice, drill once." If you drill the hole in the wrong place, not only have you wasted your time and possibly the time of others, but you just wasted the piece of lumber! So always analyze what needs to be done, seek advice from others who know that subject well, and make the right decision.

One of the Scout Laws is that a Scout is thrifty. This is one area in which people seem to make the worst decisions. Why is that? Well, it usually comes down to greed. People want more money and valuables, so they are more willing to make the wrong decisions in order to get more money. But when it comes to proper management of your finances, there are no shortcuts. Making sure that you have a proper income coming in the door and that your expenses are properly controlled requires good old-fashioned hard work.

The principle of the Navy SEALs is especially relevant in your finances. If you are making a decision related to your finances, and you don't do the right thing, it can create a situation where your financial situation can spiral out of control. For example, trying to take advantage of a "get rich quick scheme" can often put you in an immediate financial problem. And that situation can spiral out of control, making it harder and harder to get your finances under control.

In all things, you should always strive to do the right thing. But in your finances, it becomes especially important. Be thrifty and make the right decisions!

A SCOUT IS BRAVE #1

NEVER, NEVER, NEVER GIVE UP

How many of you have heard of Winston Churchill? Winston Churchill was one of the most famous leaders in the world. During World War II, he was the leader of Great Britain. Early in the war, Hitler defeated France and took over almost the entire continent of Europe. At this point, he turned his forces on the last remaining power, Great Britain.

Where was the United States? We hadn't come into the war. The memories of World War I were too strong. Most Americans felt like we shouldn't get involved in this European war. After the war, it came out that Hitler had already drafted plans to attack the United States. All that stood in his way was the tiny island of Great Britain.

Hitler launched what would later come to be known as The Battle of Britain. Hitler's plan was to decimate Great Britain with his superior air force, known as the Luftwaffe. Once he eliminated their ability to protect their island with their air force, Hitler and the Nazis could then launch an invasion of Britain across the English Channel. But Hitler hadn't counted on three things: the bravery of the English pilots, an invention called radar that enabled the British to know when the German planes were arriving, and a man named Winston Churchill. He rallied the British people, he inspired them to believe that they could defeat the Nazis, and he convinced them that they should never give up.

After the war, when he returned to his childhood school at Harrow, Winston Churchill was asked how he and the British people had defeated the Germans. What he said was simple. He said, "Never give in, never, never, never, never—in nothing, great or small, large or petty—never give in." Over the years, that phrase got shortened to "Never, never, never give up."

In life, you will be faced with constant challenges. In your schoolwork, in your sports, in your friendships, and in Scouts, people will tell you that you should give up. You will be tempted to quit. But one of the points of the Scout Law is that a Scout is brave. Brave doesn't have to mean a soldier who rushes into combat. It doesn't have to mean a policeman who chases down a drug dealer. It doesn't have to mean a firefighter who goes into a burning building to save a life.

No, bravery for you is battling those challenges that you face. It is resisting temptation. It's not doing something wrong just because, "Everyone else is doing it." It's looking adversity right in the face and doing the right thing. And it's hanging in there when the easy thing to do would be to cut and run. But, in life, it's not the quitters who become a success. It's the ones who heed the advice of Winston Churchill. "Never, never, never give up."

A SCOUT IS BRAVE #2

HE WHO FEARS HAS ALREADY LOST

A wise philosopher named Michel de Montaigne once said, "He who fears he shall suffer, already suffers what he fears."

Is it wrong to have fear? No. That's the way we are wired. When God created us, he programed us to naturally experience fear. Psychiatrists call this "fight or flee." In the early days of humans, they didn't have the technology to control all of the animals of the world. So, when humans came into contact with an animal or other foe that was more powerful than them, they had to make a decision. Do you run away to live another day, or do you stay and fight it out? But in either case, a natural fear gripped humans. In many cases, this fear was helpful. It raises the reflexes. It caused the body to release adrenaline, which increased our speed, strength, and focus. So, a little fear is good.

One of our Scout Laws is, "A Scout is Brave." Bravery can be defined as doing what is right even when our natural fear causes us not to do it. Under normal fear, bravery can be challenging, but it can be done. Let's go back to the fight or flee instinct. Let's say that you encounter a bully who demands that you give him your lunch money. You have two choices. First, you can fight. Now, I don't mean a "put up your dukes" kind of fight. Physical violence isn't the right answer. But there are other things that you can do. You could tell the bully that you aren't going to give in to him and that if he ever attempts to bully you again, you will go to the authorities.

Or, you can flee. I'm not talking about running away screaming and crying. I'm talking about calmly walking away while defusing the situation. Both of these are natural examples of normal fear and reacting in a cool, calm way.

But what Mr. Montaigne was talking about is a fear that exceeds the natural fear that we should have. He was talking about an overwhelming fear that paralyzes us and prevents us from doing what we need to do. Psychiatrists call this overwhelming fear "paranoia." When we have this overwhelming fear, it goes beyond a normal, temporary fear that we experience for a brief period of time. For example, when the bully is no longer on the scene, we return to our normal way of life. But with paranoia and other consuming fear, it controls our lives. It causes us to do things we wouldn't normally do. And many of those things might be the wrong types of things to do. At that point, the world of fear in which we live becomes worse than the original fear that we had.

There is an old bit of advice that I will leave with you that describes how to be brave and not to give in to a life of unwanted fear. It's called the Serenity Prayer. It goes like this: "God grant me the serenity to accept the things I cannot change; courage to change the things I can; and wisdom to know the difference." If you spend your time worrying about the things that you cannot change, you will develop a fear that will control your life. Recognize those for what they are and let the little, normal fears of life make you stronger and smarter.

A SCOUT IS BRAVE #3

THE WAR IS NOT LOST

After World War I, France decided that they would never be invaded by Germany again. So, they built a massive wall between their two countries. It was called the Maginot Line. It was seven stories with most of those stories underground. It had massive guns, tunnels that connected it, living quarters, hospitals, and huge eating areas. There was just one problem. All of the guns pointed toward Germany. So, when World War II began, the German army simply went through Belgium, the country to the north of France, circled around and captured Paris, the capital of France, without the guns of the Maginot Line firing a shot.

Things looked bad for France. The government of France surrendered. Most of the military surrendered. Adolf Hitler came to Paris and danced at the base of the famous Eiffel Tower. With the United States not yet in the war, this left only Great Britain to stand up against the Nazis controlling all of Europe.

But not everyone surrendered. A French general named Charles de Gaulle escaped to Great Britain with what was left of the French army. In a very famous statement, de Gaulle said, "France may have lost the battle. But France has not lost the war." France, under de Gaulle, continued to fight. Inspired by de Gaulle and his refusal to give up, citizens in France who were under German control began to band together and formed the French Underground. They blew up railroad tracks, ambushed German convoys, and generally made life miserable for the German army occupying France.

On D-Day, the United States, Britain, Canada, and other Allied countries, including France, landed on the beaches of Normandy. Who walked ashore to lead the French army? Charles de Gaulle. Realizing that de Gaulle served as an inspiration to the French people, General de Gaulle led the Allied troops in the liberation of Paris. de Gaulle went on to become one of the greatest presidents in French history. If you fly into Paris, you will land, where else? At Charles de Gaulle Airport.

Can we use the example of de Gaulle's statement in our life? Yes. In life, we will fight many battles. We will lose many of them. But do we let those battles get us down? If we do, we will lose the war.

A Scout is brave. That means that we realize in life, we are in it for the long run. For example, you could get a bad grade on one paper in school. You lost that battle. But you don't give in and assume that that class is wrecked for the whole school term. No. Like Charles de Gaulle, you know that, even though you lost the battle, you haven't lost the war. Be brave. Attack the issue head-on. Figure out why you got a bad grade. Did you not study enough? Did you study the wrong thing? Do you need to get some help with that subject? Do what you have to do. And you will win the war.

Remember, although you may lose the battle, that doesn't mean that you have lost the war. Be brave. Rebound. Adapt. Do what it takes to get back on track. And you will win the war.

A SCOUT IS BRAVE #4

TURNING OVER YOUR FIELD

There's an old Irish proverb that says, "You'll never plow a field by turning it over in your mind." You all know what it means to plow a field. Every farmer has to do this before they can plant their crops. But do you know what it means to turn something over in your mind? It means to think about it, and think about it some more, and think about it some more. In other words, what the proverb is saying is that if you keep turning something over and over in your mind, you'll never get it done.

There's a saying that you have probably heard. It was used by the military when they used to stand in long lines to fire their muskets. They don't do that anymore. Today, soldiers don't need to be ordered to all fire at once. But in the old days, like the American Revolutionary War, their guns were so inaccurate that the only way that they could shoot effectively was if everyone in line fired at the same time. So, you've heard the phrase, "Ready, aim, fire."

There was once a family who owned a business. One of the brothers was described by someone as being "Ready, fire, aim." In other words, he always seemed to fire his gun, or take action, before he had aimed, or given the matter the proper amount of thought. But the other brother was described as "Ready, aim, aim, aim…" In other words, that brother never took action. He was like the farmer who turned things over in his mind, but never got around to plowing.

In the Scout Law, we are told to be brave. But what does turning things over and over in our mind have to do with being brave? Well, what's the number one reason that somebody might keep thinking about something and thinking about it and thinking about it, rather than taking action? Fear. Fear can grip all of us. And it causes us to freeze up. All we can do in our panic is to try to figure out what we can do. But for many of us, instead of actually doing something, the fear causes us to simply keep thinking about it. Oftentimes, we simply make the situation worse by not having the bravery to take the action that we need to take.

So, in life, when you are faced with an adverse situation, don't do like the farmer who keeps turning the situation over and over in their mind. Be like the farmer who places the plow in the ground and begins doing what he needs to do. When you are faced with an adverse situation, think about what needs to be done. And then do it. That's what bravery is all about.

A SCOUT IS BRAVE #5

WORRY IS LIKE A ROCKING CHAIR

One of the best humorists was Erma Bombeck. In an era where comedians and humorists were mostly men, and women were supposed to be reserved, prim, and proper, Erma Bombeck was known as one of the funniest people.

Ms. Bombeck once said, "Worry is like a rocking chair: It gives you something to do but never gets you anywhere."

One of the Scout Laws is a Scout is brave. There are many ways to show bravery. It can be the soldier on the field of combat. It can be the person who stands up to a life-threatening disease such as cancer. It can be the person who falls off the horse, but is brave enough to climb back on the horse.

One of the biggest challenges to bravery is worry. Have you ever met what is called a worry wart? We all know what a wart is. It's that thing that grows on your hand or other body part, and you just can't seem to get rid of it. Well, a worry wart is sort of like that. They grow and expand. They never seem to go away. They just seem to put a damper on everything.

Does life give us plenty of things to worry about? Sure. But in order to be brave, we need to be able to get past that worry. One of the most influential statements is to not worry about things that you can't control. Let's say that you have a big activity coming up. Maybe it's the high school prom. Maybe it's a big athletic event. Maybe it's a date with that special person. But a few days before the event, you hear that the weather is going to be bad. It's going to rain cats and dogs. You have two ways to approach it. First, you can worry yourself about it. You can lose sleep. You can lose your focus on important things. You can be worried about something you can't control.

Or you can take the opposite approach. Just go buy an umbrella! There are lots of things about being brave that are very, very difficult. But simply not allowing the minor things in life to cause you to worry is not one of them. Change the things for the better that you can change. But don't be a worry wart. Don't worry about things that you can't change. Just go with the flow!

A SCOUT IS CLEAN #1

YOU ARE IN CONTROL OF YOUR LIFE

One of the Scout Laws is that a Scout is clean. Does that mean that we should be constantly taking a bath? I suppose that piece of advice could be good. If you have ever shared a tent with someone, you know that there's nothing wrong with good hygiene.

But the claim that is referred to in the Scout Law is something different. It is referring to having good morals. Although the twelve points of the Scout Law are all good, there are not too many of them that are mentioned in both the Scout Oath and the Scout Law. Good morals is one of them. In the Scout Oath, it tells us to be morally straight. In the Scout Law, it tells us to be clean.

So, what is one of the ways that we can live a life that is morally clean? There are lots of pieces of good advice that come from notable people. Noted entrepreneur, author, and motivational speaker, Michael Altshuler, once said: "The bad news is time flies. The good news is you're the pilot."

What exactly does that mean? Well, we all know the saying that time flies. It simply means that time seems to go by quickly. And the older you get, the more time seems to fly by. But the author is using a little play on words. The word fly also refers to flying an airplane. Airplanes need a pilot. They are the ones who control the plane. So, what the author is referring to is that you are the pilot of the time that you spend here on earth. In other words, you are in control.

Since you are the pilot, and you are in control, you make the decisions that determine how your life is lived. Throughout life, you will make many decisions regarding your morals. Morals are the way that you live your life. You can make good moral decisions, or you can make bad moral decisions. You are the pilot. You are in control. Since living a good moral life is mentioned twice in the precepts for Scouting, in the Oath and in the Laws, this one is doubly important. As you live your life, remember that you are the pilot. You are in control. Don't let others convince you that you need to make bad decisions. Take ownership of everything you do. And always make the good and honorable moral decisions.

A SCOUT IS CLEAN #2

KNOWING WHAT TO DO AND ACTUALLY DOING IT

When thinking of the most famous generals in American history, we tend to think back on military leaders from long ago. We think of people such as George Washington, Robert E. Lee, or Ulysses S. Grant. But one of the most successful generals of all time came from more recent history. General Norman Schwarzkopf was the commander of the American and coalition forces during the Gulf War.

General Schwarzkopf once said, "The truth of the matter is that you always know the right thing to do. The hard thing is doing it."

It seems like when someone does something that they shouldn't do, one of their most common excuses is, "But I didn't know what to do." But is that really the case? Deep down inside, did they really not know what was the right thing to do? I think a more common scenario is that that person knew exactly what they should do. The problem was that they didn't want to do it.

Doing the right thing is often difficult. Peer pressure is a very strong influence in your life. Nobody wants to be seen as a coward. Nobody wants to be seen as a "goody two shoes." So, the majority of the time they know the right decision to make, or the right thing to do, they're just scared to do it.

One of the Scout Laws is a Scout is clean. We all know that that has nothing to do with taking a bath! Don't get me wrong, that's a good thing to do. Your friends and fellow Scouts will appreciate it! The Scout Law that says that a Scout is clean refers to the moral decisions that Scouts make. Your moral behavior has been formed in many ways. As a small child, your parents contributed to teaching you the right things. While many television programs, movies, books, and video games specialize in giving bad moral teachings to people in an effort to make a buck, most movies and other forms of entertainment still have "a happy ending." And usually, that happy ending comes when someone does the right thing.

Your religious teachings may also contribute to your knowledge of morals. And, at the end of the day, there is that tiny little voice within all of us, called our conscience, that tells us the difference between right and wrong. The next time you face a moral decision, go with the clean approach. Analyze the situation. Determine what is the right thing to do. And then stick with your moral fiber. Friends may question your activity at first. But in the long run, they are more likely to respect you more if you stick to your moral guidance.

A SCOUT IS CLEAN #3

BE TRUE TO YOURSELF

If I was to say to you, "Tonight, we are going to read some Shakespeare," some of you might think that that was pretty cool. Others might give out a little groan. But the fact of the matter is that, outside of the Bible, the number one selling author of all time is William Shakespeare. He is generally thought of as being the greatest playwright of all time. His works such as *Macbeth, Romeo and Juliet,* and *Hamlet* are considered to be some of the finest plays ever written.

But in addition to being entertaining, Mr. Shakespeare also had some pretty good advice in his plays. In the play *Hamlet*, Polonius is giving fatherly advice to his son, Laertes. He says: "This above all: to thine own self be true, and it must follow, as the night the day, thou canst not then be false to any man."

One of the Scout Laws is that a Scout is clean. We generally think of that as making good moral decisions. Avoiding certain bad things on the internet. Not gossiping. Thinking clean thoughts about yourself and others. But there is another angle to being clean. And that is the element of honesty. Whether we're dealing with a little white lie or a whopper of a tall tale, being honest to yourself and to your friends is critically important.

According to Mr. Shakespeare, what is the best way to be honest to others? Well, it starts with being honest with yourself. The funny thing about it is that you know when you're not being honest. Let's say that there is some information that your best friend needs to know. Maybe it's something that they can perform better. Maybe it's something that affects their schoolwork, their athletic performance, their job, or even their love life. Although you know that it is best to provide them with this information, you think to yourself, "It's better if I don't hurt their feelings."

In this case, you're simply not being honest with yourself. But at least you know that you're not being honest! What about all the times that you're not honest with other people? Think of all the damage that you can do.

So, take some advice from Mr. Shakespeare. Start off with being honest with yourself. If you're able to be honest with yourself, you will go a long, long way toward training yourself to be honest with other people. Honesty is like a habit. It's formed by repeating something over and over again. If you continue to lie to yourself, it makes it easy to lie to others. But if you're honest with yourself, it makes it so much easier to the honest with others.

A SCOUT IS CLEAN #4

DON'T TAKE THE BAIT

Have you ever been fishing, and like a good environmentally conscious Scout, you were throwing the fish back into the pond? But then you caught a fish that looked amazingly familiar. You just knew that that was one of the fish that you had already caught. Perhaps you wondered to yourself, why don't fish learn from their experiences? They shouldn't fall for that one again.

Well, that's the difference between you and a fish. As a human, you have the intellect to be able to learn from your experiences. Sure, we can fall for something similar more than once. You might have heard the old saying, "Fool me once, shame on you. Fool me twice, shame on me." Thankfully, most of us have enough sense not to do the same thing wrong twice in a row.

One of our most famous presidents, Thomas Jefferson, had something to say regarding biting the hook. Mr. Jefferson said, "Do not bite at the bait of pleasure until you know there is no hook beneath it."

Mr. Jefferson wasn't talking about biting the same hook twice. What he was referring to was being careful to find out what lies beneath that tasty little morsel. And this has a lot to do with the Scout Law that a Scout is clean.

Have you ever noticed that the things that get us in trouble seem to offer us a lot of pleasure? We don't engage in immoral sexual activities like surfing the internet because it's painful. We don't gossip and talk behind people's backs because it's an unpleasant experience. We don't cheat on a test because it offers a chance of bringing us pain. No, we do it because it offers us the potential pleasure of fooling everyone into thinking that we got a good grade.

You've all heard the phrase, "It's too good to be true." Well, if a temptation comes before you, and the pleasure that it offers seems too good to be true, that's probably the case. Look over the situation carefully. Peel back the layers like you would an onion. See what lies underneath. Is there a hook lurking beneath the surface that will make our experience of temporary pleasure into one of long-term pain? Don't be afraid to be a little cautious when you encounter something that wants to reward you for doing something that you probably shouldn't. Don't be afraid to just say no.

A SCOUT IS CLEAN #5

WHAT REALLY COUNTS IS WHAT YOU DO WHEN NO ONE IS WATCHING

One of the greatest college basketball coaches of all time was John Wooden. Most people would measure the greatness of a coach by their winning record and the number of championships they won. If that's the yardstick you use, John Wooden would be right at the top. His UCLA Bruins won more national championships than any other college team.

But John Wooden chose to measure himself in other ways. He measured himself based on the impact that he had on the lives of his players and those around them. He gave his players many words of advice that had nothing to do with playing basketball, but had to do with playing the game of life. One of the things that he said was, "Be more concerned with your character than your reputation, because your character is what you really are, while your reputation is merely what others think you are."

We all develop a reputation. It can be a good reputation or a bad reputation. But as Coach Wooden said, your reputation can only be based on the things that people see and hear you say and do. What they can't see is what you are thinking.

Coach Wooden had something to say about that also. He said, "To be true to yourself means having integrity. It means doing the right thing even when no one is looking."

Think about it. How can something add to or subtract from someone's reputation if no one sees it? It's easy to fool people by saying and doing the right thing when you are in front of them. But the Scout Law tells us that a Scout is clean. Are we really being clean and a person of high integrity if we're only being clean when we are in front of someone else?

No. A life of integrity is better defined by what we do when no one else is around. What are you doing on the computer when no one is around to see? Is it right to steal a look at someone else's test paper, even when you know that no one can see what you're doing? Is it right to think horrible things about someone else, even when those images are trapped in your brain, unable to be viewed by anyone else?

I'm afraid that living a clean life is much more challenging than just worrying about what you do in front of others. It has to do with what you do all the time. But here's a good suggestion. The next time you're by yourself and you're tempted to do something wrong, imagine you're in front of an audience of a hundred people. Maybe that will help you do the right thing!

A SCOUT IS REVERENT #1

THE LIGHT THAT YOU FOLLOW

Scouting recognizes that Scouts around the world have many different religions. So, the program does not try to dictate to a Scout which religion they must follow. The Scouting program simply requires that a young person acknowledge that there is a Creator.

However, regardless of which religion you follow, there is one thing that is common with all religions. That is the belief that the Creator is in charge. While mankind, in its rebellious way, has tried numerous times to put the Creator aside and give full power and authority to humans, all religions stress that that will not work. God continues to be in control. Many religions put this in different ways. However, it is very well summarized in Psalm 119:105:

"Your word is a lamp to my feet and a light for my path."

What does it mean when we say that your word is a lamp to my feet and a light for my path? The word refers to all of the writings and other information that our religions' Creators left for us. In some religions, the word actually refers to the deity themselves. But in each religion, the Creator has provided a way to show us the way that we should proceed through life. They have provided guidance for what we should do and not do. If you have ever tried to stumble through a dark house without light, you know how difficult and painful that can be. A flashlight or a lamp in the old days provided the light needed to find one's way. That's exactly what the Creator does. Their word serves as the lamp that lights our way.

But there is something important to note in that sentence. Many people believe that they light their own path. In other words, the path that they take and the way in which they see that path is determined solely by them. This verse makes it quite clear. It is the Creator who lights our path and determines in which direction we should go.

Obviously, we will make many decisions throughout our life that determine which direction we go. An example would be where we decide to go to school. Or what job we decide to do. Or where we decide to live. Or with whom we decide to live. But that's not what this verse is referring to. When this verse refers to the path, it is referring to the total path. Our path is our entire life from start to finish. Granted, we will make many important decisions along the way. But the path itself and the direction that we must follow can only come from the Creator.

The Scout Law tells us that we are to be reverent. Reverent means to follow the words of the Creator. In following the words of the Creator, remember that they will provide the light in our life and show us the path upon which we should proceed.

A SCOUT IS REVERENT #2

ADVERSITY MAKES US STRONGER

Regardless of which religion you belong to, there is one thing that is common to all. Our God, or Creator, or Supreme Being, or whatever term you use, does not make you immune to all adversity. In fact, adversity is a part of our life. It is actually a critical part of how we grow as believers.

Different religions say it differently. But I think 1 Chronicles 29:17 summarizes how it works:

"I know, my God, that you test the heart and are pleased with integrity."

Not only does God allow bad things to happen to good people, but he actively uses adversity to make us stronger. In this verse, we read that God "tests the heart." What does that mean? Well, we all know what a test is. We have to take them in school all of the time. Are they pleasant? Well, some people like the challenge of having someone test their knowledge. For them, a math test is kind of like a trivia contest. But for most of us, I think it is fair to say that we don't really like to take tests.

It's interesting to look at the origin of the word test. It comes from the Latin word, testa. Testa is the Latin word for a small clay pot. So, how did we get from a small pot to a dreaded math exam? Well, when you are extracting valuable minerals, chemicals, and other products, people would put what they had dug up in a small pot. They would then heat up the pot. The excess dirt and other materials would be burned off. And what would remain was the valuable material.

When we are tested in life, it's a lot like that process. God applies the heat so that we are able to burn off the bad things in our life. And what emerges is the good stuff. A stronger person.

Here's another way to look at it. Have you ever watched a blacksmith? What do they do to forge hard steel? The burn it. They put it in an oven where it is heated to extraordinary temperatures. The bad stuff is burned off. And what emerges is the strong stuff.

So, the next time you face adversity, you can whine and complain about it. You can ask God, "What did I do to deserve this?" Or, you can thank God for placing you in the fire. Be it in the small clay pot, or in the blacksmith's oven. God places you in the fire to make you stronger.

Our Scout Law says that a Scout is reverent. The next time you are tested, remember that that is God's way of burning off the bad stuff and making you stronger.

A SCOUT IS REVERENT #3

SERVICE TO OTHERS

The last of the Scout Laws is that a Scout is reverent. While different religions may have different interpretations of their God or Supreme Being, there is one thing that is true of them all. And that is that as believers, we are to serve our fellow man. Oftentimes, this service can come with a price. We might be required to give up something that we like or like to do in order to take the time, energy, or expense to help out someone less fortunate than ourselves.

But you will find that your reward for a life of service can come in many different forms. Let me illustrate with a story. Two travelers were trudging through the cold and the snow. They were trying to get to their destination before nightfall, knowing that if they were caught out in the open after dark, they would surely perish. But as they neared the village, they came across a wounded traveler. The traveler lay half-frozen on the side of the road.

The first traveler said, "It is this man's fate to die here. Therefore, I must continue on my way before I die here also."

However, the other traveler said, "My faith requires me to help this man. As dangerous as it may be to me, I cannot simply walk away and leave this man to die. My God is a compassionate God and asks me to be the same." So, the second traveler picked up the wounded man and put him over his shoulder. The wounded traveler was heavy. He slowed down the progress of the second traveler, who found himself falling behind the first traveler. Many times, he wanted to lay down the wounded man and forge on to the village before nightfall. But he trudged ahead.

Finally, in the distance, he spotted the lights of the village. But as he neared the front of the gates, he stumbled over something in his path. It was his fellow traveler, frozen to death just short of the gate. But the exertion of carrying the wounded man had kept him warm. He arrived safely in the village, where the wounded traveler was nursed back to health. While the traveler did not realize what was happening, he realized later that God rewarded him for his service to his fellow man.

I hope that none of you are caught out on the trail on a cold freezing night. But I hope that you remember the story of the two travelers. God has asked us to give to others. It may be food or other support for the poor. It may be a kind word to a stranger. It may be a helping hand to one of your friends. Don't always go into that situation expecting some dramatic reward for your service. Simply go into that situation of service because it's the right thing to do.

A SCOUT IS REVERENT #4

SANDCASTLES ALWAYS WASH AWAY

Have you ever built a sandcastle on the beach? If so, you know that there's one thing that is true. When you come back to the beach the next morning, the sandcastle will be gone. Why is that? It's because of the tides. You've all heard of gravity. That's the force that causes an object that you dropped from your hand to fall to the ground. The rotation of an object such as the earth creates a force called gravity. That force pulls objects toward the rotating star or planet.

You might have heard the story of how a scientist named Isaac Newton figured out gravity when an apple fell on his head. We aren't really sure if the apple fell on his head. Or he just watched it fall. And we aren't sure that he "figured out" why gravity works. But at least he discovered how it works.

Believe it or not, high tides and low tides are caused by the gravitational pull of the moon. You would think that the moon is so far away that it wouldn't be able to pull objects toward it. But it does, and as the earth rotates, the pull of the moon causes the waves of the ocean to rise and fall. When the waves rise high, it is called a high tide. When the waves recede, it is called a low tide. And it never changes. No matter how beautiful that sandcastle is, the high tide will always come in and wash it away.

If you think about it, the sandcastle is a thing of man. It is built by mortal man. But the waves come from God. And like many things of God, they are far more powerful than the things of man.

But there's another thing about the tides. They never change! The things of mankind can change. Our rulers can change. Our civilizations can come and go. Our fashions and other fads can change in a matter of years. But the things of God never change. Things like the love of God never change. God's grace and mercy never change. God's plan for the universe never changes.

One of the Scout Laws is that a Scout is reverent. That means that you are placing your belief in a higher power. Would you put your faith in something that is constantly changing? No. You want the confidence that if you place your faith in something, it will remain unchanging. Gravitation and the tides that it causes will never change. The tide will always win the battle with the sandcastle. God is like that tide. God will never change, and God will always win the battle.

A SCOUT IS REVERENT #5

GRACE

One of the finest American religious writers is Kevin Moore. He made an interesting observation about comfort in one of his books. He said: "Comfort is not the absence of problems but the grace to experience life in the midst of them."

One of the age-old questions that people ask is, "Why would a loving God allow people to suffer?" Regardless of your religion, the common factor is that each religion believes in a higher power. They might be called different names. The stories of their actions might very. But religions are all consistent in their belief in a higher power. In all religions, this higher power has the ability to affect those things that take place around us. They cause us to be born. They cause us to die. They have the ability to control what happens to us during our lives.

But when something goes wrong and we find ourselves in an uncomfortable position, the inevitable question is, "Why is this happening to me?" Inevitably, we wonder why God has not protected us from adversity.

One of the Scout Laws is a Scout is reverent. Have there been and are there now Scouts who, in fact, have not believed in a higher power? The answer to this is, of course. People can say and do the things that they feel like others want them to say and do in order to be part of something. I can't search your heart to determine what your relationship is with the Creator. But regardless of your belief structure, odds are good that you have found yourself questioning the Creator as to why they allow bad things to happen to good people.

In all things, we want comfort. But comfort can be described in many different ways. What Pastor Moore is saying is that comfort doesn't have to be a complete lack of adverse situations. In fact, it is a given that we are going to face adverse conditions. We're going to get sick. We're going to be in car wrecks. We're going to get rejected by other people. We're going to lose our loved ones. And one day, we are all going to pass away. Our Creator, though, doesn't necessarily will those things to happen. But rather, the Creator may simply be allowing them to happen. Why? Because that's how the Creator strengthens us. Just like fire tempers steel. The adversity that we face causes us to be stronger.

So, it's not the lack of adversity that determines our level of comfort. Rather, our ability to deal with and to accept adversity is what will determine how comfortable we are in life. I'm not saying that we have to be the tough guy, showing no emotion. But we need to recognize adversity for what it is. And, through grace, have the strength and faith to overcome that adversity.

ON MY HONOR #1

A MATTER OF CHARACTER

One of the most influential writers of recent time is John Maxwell. He has written numerous books on how to be the best person we can be. John Maxwell once said, "Talent is a gift, but character is a choice."

We have all seen people with great talent. Turn on the television any weekend, and you will see people with incredible athletic ability. Go to a movie or a play, and you will see people with an amazing talent for acting. Go to a high school or college graduation, and you will see people with all kinds of sashes and knots, indicating their academic talent.

Where does this amazing talent come from? Well, ultimately, it comes from God. It may be manifested in the form of genes and things inherited from one's parents. It can be nourished by that talented person. Or it can be wasted. The history of mankind is full of examples where someone wasted their talent. But if they take their God-given talent and nourish it, build upon it, and make the most of it, it is truly a gift.

But as John Maxwell says, character is a choice. I suppose some character flaws can be attributed to genes or how we are wired. Good or bad character can be influenced by our surroundings. Do we grow up with parents who teach us right and wrong? Do we choose friends who provide a positive influence on us or a negative influence?

But at the end of the day, character is still a choice that we make. Regardless of whether our parents spend time teaching us the difference between right and wrong, we still inherently know what is right and wrong. Society provides us with a moral code. For most of us, our religion teaches us moral values. But for most of us, our conscience teaches us right and wrong. For example, regardless of your religious beliefs, it is generally accepted as a norm of society that one does not kill another person.

But even if our parents have taught us well, if our religion has defined the difference between good and bad, and if that tiny little voice inside of us tells us if there is something that we should not be doing, it still comes down to a moment of truth. You may have seen the little cartoon where a person has an angel on one shoulder and a devil on the other. Both are whispering in the ear of that person. Do they do the right thing? Or do they do the wrong thing?

And that's where character comes into play. The first line of the Scout Oath is "On my honor." Honor is choosing to do the right thing. Honor is choosing to show good character. Honor is realizing when we are being tempted to do the wrong thing, but overcoming that temptation and doing the right thing. It's important to note that the Scout Oath says "On MY honor." When making a choice, it isn't anybody else's honor that's on the line. It's yours. Make sure to make the right choices.

ON MY HONOR #2

BOBBY JONES AND THE PENALTY

Bobby Jones was one of the greatest golfers of all time. He was a huge influence on golf in its early days. He was the first golfer to win all of the major golf tournaments. And he is the only golfer ever to win them all in one year. In one of his most lasting achievements, Bobby Jones launched the tournament that we now know as The Masters Tournament.

But perhaps the largest example that Bobby Jones left was that of sportsmanship. Virtually every other sport has umpires or referees who called penalties on the players. Many athletes will admit that they break the rules in hopes that they don't get caught by the officials. But golf is different. In golf, the players call penalties on themselves. And this is an example set by Bobby Jones.

In the 1925 U. S. Open, Bobby Jones hit his ball into the tall grass, called the rough, on the eleventh hole. As he took a practice swing, his ball grazed the grass around the ball, causing the ball to move. But no one saw it except Bobby Jones. Bobby Jones immediately informed his playing partner, Walter Hagen, that his ball had moved. Walter Hagen said that he had not seen it move and encouraged Bobby to play on as if nothing had happened. Bobby Jones informed the tournament officials that he had accidentally moved his ball. Again, they said that no one else had seen the ball move, and encouraged him not to take a penalty, but to continue to play on. Bobby Jones simply said that no one else might have seen his ball move, but he had. And that was all it took for him to do the right thing and call a penalty upon himself. Ironically, Bobby Jones went on to lose this major tournament by one stroke!

The Scout Oath says that we are to act "on my honor." Doing things with honor means to do the right thing. But for many of us, our definition of doing the right thing only includes doing that when someone else will notice whether we do the right thing or the wrong thing. You might be tempted to do the right thing when you are being watched. But what if you knew that you could cheat on a test in school and probably get away with? What would you do? Well, if you were Bobby Jones, it wouldn't matter. You would still do the right thing, even if nobody else knew about it.

As a Scout, I hope you will take an example from Bobby Jones. It may not be as dramatic as losing a major golf tournament by one stroke if you call a penalty on yourself for something that nobody else noticed. But just remember, even if nobody else notices what you do, you know.

DO MY BEST #1

LETTING GO

Lao Tzu was an ancient philosopher and the founder of the religion of Taoism. He once said the following: "When I let go of what I am, I become what I might be."

What does it mean to let go of what I am in order to become what I might be? Well, you're probably familiar with the butterfly and what happens during what is called metamorphosis. They go from the egg, to the larva, to the pupa, and then to the butterfly. Have you ever seen a butterfly egg? It's not very attractive. The larva and the pupa aren't much to look at either. But butterflies are some of the most beautiful things on the earth. How does the butterfly move through the stages to become a beautiful animal? By letting go of their current state and moving on to their next state.

If the butterfly could somehow prevent this natural process from happening, they would never become their best. They would never become the beautiful butterfly. Interestingly though, we as humans go through a similar physical growth pattern. We move from the egg, to the fetus, to the baby, to the teenager, to the adult. Just like the butterfly, it is impossible for us to prevent our natural growth.

But while we can't prevent the physical growth, we can impede our mental and psychological growth. When you were born, you are like a sponge. You're soaking up knowledge of the things around you. But as we progress into our teenage and adult years, the burden for us to learn and gain knowledge falls more on ourselves. We could make the bad decision to drop out of high school in order to get a low-paying job. We could turn down the opportunity to go to college or a technical school to learn more and to be able to become more of a contributor in society. We could choose not to listen to our parents or teachers or other people of authority.

Throughout life, you will be presented with opportunities to learn and become a better person. Many people choose not to give up where they are at. They look at change as always being bad, scary, difficult, or challenging. But if we are unwilling to let go of where we are in order to move ahead in life, we are like a marathon runner running on a treadmill. We are using up lots of energy, but we are not going anywhere.

Life will give you many opportunities to improve yourself. The Scout Oath says that we are supposed to do our best. Doing your best often requires you to change from what you're currently doing, learn how to do better, and have the courage to learn new ways to do things. The next time an opportunity to improve yourself approaches you, don't just dismiss it as too hard, scary, or risky. Give it careful consideration. If you need to, discuss it with your parents, teacher, Scout leader, or someone of authority. Remember, many things might look good, but someone of experience can point out things that are sometimes too good to be true. Once you determine that it's a great opportunity, give it a try! But always remember that in order for the beautiful butterfly to be created, it has to give up where it's at and go somewhere different.

DO MY BEST #2

NEVER GIVE UP

Most of you have probably heard a story of how Thomas Edison invented the light bulb. You've heard how he tried ten thousand different possible filaments, the substance within the bulb itself that gives off the light, before he found the right material for the filament. Well, first let me correct a little myth. Thomas Edison actually didn't invent the light bulb. Believe it or not, there were over twenty different light bulbs invented before Thomas Edison created his light bulb. But none of the light bulbs were very effective. The filament in the light bulb burnt out quickly. You would be constantly changing the light bulb in your lamp. What Thomas Edison did was to invent the filament that caused the light bulb to burn for many, many hours before it had to be changed. So, you would be correct in saying that Thomas Edison invented the first light bulb that could be a commercial success.

When thinking about what Thomas Edison did, and the patience that he showed, two quotes come to mind. First, when someone asked him how it felt to fail so many times, Edison responded, "I have not failed. I've just found 10,000 ways that won't work."

But Edison had more to say about failure and giving up. He also said, "Many of life's failures are people who did not realize how close they were to success when they gave up."

Can you imagine what life would've been like if Thomas Edison had given up after filament experiment number 9,999? We might all be sitting here in the dark! Actually, I'm sure that somebody else would have come along and invented the light bulb. But there would've been a whole lot of people sitting in the dark for a much longer period of time.

The Scout Oath tells us that we are to do our best. There are a lot of things we can say about doing our best. But, one of the most important things is not to give up. There are many reasons why people give up. First, could be our natural impatience. People simply get tired or bored with something and want to move on. Another reason might be distractions. Life is full of all types of distractions. Things are constantly trying to get our attention and call us to drop what we were doing in order to move on to something else.

I hate to say it, but laziness could be involved. If we are facing a hard task, it can often be easy just to decide that we don't want to do the work necessary to finish that task. It could be that we don't know what we need to do to finish the task. No one could tell Edison what the missing filament should be. He couldn't go to a book or to the internet to find out the answer. So, not knowing what to do can definitely cause us to give up on a task.

But what does the Scout Oath tell us to do? It tells us to do our best. Your best doesn't mean giving up on a task. It means carrying that task through to completion. It's especially important to finish a task if someone is depending on us. But even if you were simply doing that task for yourself, it's still very important to be true to yourself, give it your best, and carry that task through to its completion.

TO DO MY DUTY #1

DON'T BE AFRAID TO STEP UP AND DO WHAT IS EXPECTED OF YOU

During World War II, the story is told about a young captain who was addressing his troops. He needed volunteers for a mission. The mission was very dangerous. Those who volunteered might not come back alive. He wanted all volunteers to take one step forward. But right after he made that request, he turned around to receive a message. When he turned back around, the line was unbroken. No one had volunteered. He began telling his men how disappointed he was in them. He said that there should be at least one of them who was brave enough to risk his life to serve his country. Finally, one brave soldier spoke up. He said, "But sir, while you were turned around, every soldier took one step forward."

Thankfully, it is doubtful that any of you will be called upon for a suicide mission. But you will all face the situation where you are asked to step up and do your duty. It might be as simple as making your bed in the morning. Or making sure to study hard the night before the big test. It might be a situation that you face in life, such as defending the honor of a friend.

In order to understand what is meant by your duty, it is helpful to look at the origin of the word. The word duty comes from the word due. What does it mean for something to be due? If you borrow money from someone, and it becomes due, that means that you have to pay them back. If you keep a library book out too long, and get hit with a fine, then it is something that is due. If someone drives their car too fast and gets a ticket, then the amount of that fine is due.

So, the word due means that it is something that must be paid. It's not an option. If we get a speeding ticket, we can't just say, "I don't think I'll pay this." We can say that, but does that mean that that fine goes away? No. It is still due. So, our duty is something that we owe to someone else. It may involve finances. For example, it is our duty to pay sales tax on something that we buy. But, most of the time, a duty is an action that we have to take.

You may have heard the term "civic duty." These are the things that we need to do in order to be part of a properly working society. Paying our property taxes is one example. Voting is another example of our civic duty. But like a speeding ticket, do we have to vote? No. Sadly, only about half of the voting age people in the U. S. vote in the average election. So, we don't have to vote, but it is our duty. It is something that we should do. Other duties might involve part of your household, classroom, or Scout troop. If it's your duty to dig the latrine on the next campout, step up and do what you need to do. Digging that latrine might seem like a suicide mission, but it's not.

So, when asked to do your duty, take one step forward and do it. Better yet, do your duty without even having to be asked.

TO DO MY DUTY #2

PERSIST IN DOING YOUR DUTY

One of the greatest writers and poets of all time was Ralph Waldo Emerson. Mr. Emerson once said, "That which we persist in doing becomes easier to do, not that the nature of the thing has changed but that our power to do has increased."

What Mr. Emerson was talking about is persistence and doing the things that we are supposed to do. His point was that the more we do something, the easier it becomes to do it. Think about something that you had to do which you knew was the right thing, but you just didn't want to do it. Let's take an example. Let's say that a friend of your parents has passed away. Your parents inform you that you are going to join them for the funeral. You whine. You complain. You really didn't know that person all that well. They were a friend of your parents, not one of your friends. Why do you have to go to the funeral?

Well, most people don't like to go to funerals. But it's the right thing to do. It's important to honor the memory of that person. It's important for that family to feel the support of friends and family at that time of need. Being there for that family who are in mourning is the right thing to do.

But do you remember what it was like the first time you went to a funeral? You might have been nervous. You might have been a little unsure about what to say to the grieving family. You might just have been a little scared of the whole process. Dealing with death or illness has never been easy.

But if you have had the opportunity to go to more than one funeral, you may have noticed that it got a little easier the second time. And maybe even a little easier the third time. As Mr. Emerson asked, "Has the nature of the thing changed?" Of course not. A funeral is still a funeral. But because we had been persistent in performing our duties, our power to perform that duty increased.

The Scout Oath says that we are to do our duty. Doing your duty does not always come easy. Like with that funeral, you may be nervous. You may be scared. You may be unsure what to say and do. But as a good Scout, that doesn't matter. Do your duty, and the process becomes easier and easier.

TO GOD AND TO MY COUNTRY #1

HAVING BUT ONE LIFE TO GIVE

How many of you have heard of Nathan Hale? If you are a student of American history, you know that Nathan Hale was a spy for George Washington's army during the American Revolutionary War. During the war, Nathan Hale, who was an otherwise unknown soldier, volunteered to go on an intelligence gathering mission. He was captured by the British soldiers. After a brief trial, he was executed by hanging. Nathan Hale was only twenty-one years old.

Nathan Hale wasn't the only spy in that war or any other war. Many other spies were captured and executed. So why is it that we remember his name? Because of the famous lines that he uttered before he was hanged. While there is some dispute among historians as to exactly what he said, the generally accepted quote is, "I only regret that I have but one life to give for my country."

Imagine for a moment that you are a twenty-one-year-old soldier. You are captured by the most formidable army of its time. We can only imagine that the incarceration and trial that you suffered was humiliating and scary. Imagine what it was like to be marched up upon a scaffold to stand behind the noose that was about to snap your neck. What do you think you might've said?

I suppose that most people might have whimpered and asked their executioner for mercy. And I wouldn't blame them at all. But at that time, Nathan Hale's only thought was that if he had to do it all over again, he would. Why? Because he felt like the thing that he was doing was a noble cause that was important for the freedom of his country.

I doubt that any of you will ever find yourself in this type of position. I certainly hope that you don't. But every day, you have an opportunity to give service to God and to your country. The Scout Oath says that we are to give to God and our country. There are many ways to do this. Simply thinking positively about God and country is one way. And I certainly hope that you all will do that. But in life, you will have opportunities to go far beyond simple thoughts through your actions. They may be dramatic, like joining the military and putting your life on the line for your country. But there are many other ways that you can take action to support your country. Following the laws is a good start. Voting in our elections is another way. Supporting your public officials is another good one. These are ways that you can support your country. Nathan Hale left life regretting that he wasn't able to do more for his country. Make sure that you don't have any regrets about not doing what you can to serve God and country.

TO GOD AND COUNTRY

KEEPING THE FLAME BURNING

One of the most recognized monks was St. Francis of Assisi. Have you ever seen the statue that is in gardens of the monk with the bird on his shoulder? That was St. Francis. Among other things, he is the patron saint of animals and nature. One of the things that St. Francis said was: "All the darkness in the world cannot extinguish the light of a single candle."

Think about that one. Darkness is one of the most extensive things in the world. It permeates our houses when our lights go out. It encompasses the world for roughly half of the day. It extends out through space for as far as we know that it exists. It's a very powerful force.

But if we light a single candle, the light given out by that simple candle drives the powerful darkness away. And with all of its strength and might, the darkness is utterly powerless to extinguish that candle.

In the Scout Oath, we are reminded of our duty to God and country. Sometimes, we might be tempted to think that our country is an all-powerful force that nothing can challenge. But if you look back on the history of our country, that's not always true.

Our country started off with very dangerous intentions. Our forefathers decided to declare independence and go to war with the most powerful nation in the world, Great Britain. Unless you study your history closely, you don't realize how perilously close the colonists were to losing their attempt at independence. Virtually every historian feels like if it had not been for the intervention of our French allies, the colonists would have faced certain defeat.

Throughout our history, we have faced adverse situations when darkness threatened to encompass our country. We have faced financial issues like the Great Depression. We have faced off against major military powers, including the Nazis in World War II, the Chinese in the Korean War, and the USSR in the Cold War. And more American soldiers were killed in a war of our own making, the American Civil War, than in any other war.

And yet, in all of the darkness of those events, the candle lit by our forefathers on July 4, 1776 has remained lit. It has continued to illuminate the principles of liberty and freedom upon which our country was built.

But the candle did not stay lit by itself. Countless lives have been given in an effort to keep our country viable and moving forward. While you may not be asked to give that eternal sacrifice, it is essential that each of us offer our support to our country. We may not always agree with the politicians who happen to be in power. But we should still offer to them our support and respect. Take every opportunity you have to give back to your country. Let's all work together to keep that candle lit!

OBEY THE SCOUT LAW #1

LEARN FROM OTHERS

One of the greatest academics of all times was Joseph Campbell. He was a professor of literature. If you aren't really big on having to read great literature in school, you have Joseph Campbell to blame. He helped develop a strong interest in literature as an academic subject. Mr. Campbell once said: "Where you stumble and fall, there you will find gold."

We generally don't think of stumbling and falling as being a positive experience. But the point that Mr. Campbell was making was that we learn from our experiences. We learn from positive experiences. If we do something enjoyable, we immediately want to do it more often. But sometimes, it seems like we learn more from our negative experiences than we do from our positive experiences. If a young child accidentally places their hand over a flame, it's not a very fun thing. But they immediately learn a lesson. Flames are hot. Don't touch them.

In life, you will stumble. You will stumble a lot. But what you want to do is turn that fall into a positive experience. I'm not saying that you should pretend like it didn't happen. When you do stumble, analyze why it happened. See what you can learn from the experience. For example, if you're jogging around your neighborhood, and you come to an uneven place on the sidewalk where you stumble and fall, what can you learn from that experience? I suppose the first thing that you would learn would be that you need to lift up your feet more as you run. You might learn that you need to be looking down at the sidewalk, in addition to looking off in the distance. The bottom line is that we are going to stumble and fall.

The important thing to do is always learn from those stumbles. Which brings us to one of the points of the Scout Oath. In the Scout Oath, we are told to obey the Scout Law. The Scout Law is a collection of twelve points which we should live and demonstrate in our lives. But have you ever wondered where the twelve points of the Scout Law came from and why they are so important? Well, the Scout Law came from a whole lot of stumbles and falls. The early leaders of the Scout movement experienced many positive things in their lives. Much of the Scout program is based on these positive things such as trust, loyalty, and enjoyment of the outdoors. But another important aspect of Scouting is that these early leaders experienced stumbles in their lives. They learned from these stumbles. And what they learned was that the attributes in the Scout Law such as being trustworthy, loyal, helpful … well, you know the others, are the types of positive attributes that will make you a better person.

So, next time you take a tumble, analyze what went wrong. Learn from that negative experience. Work hard to turn it into a positive. But also learn from the stumbles and falls of the wise people who came before you. You've heard the statement, "Don't reinvent the wheel." Well, when it comes to living a positive life, there's no need to invent a wheel that one of the early Scout leaders invented!

OBEY THE SCOUT LAW #2

YOU CALL THE SHOTS

Eleanor Roosevelt was the wife of President Franklin D. Roosevelt. She is generally considered to be one of the most influential First Ladies. Eleanor Roosevelt once said, "No man or woman can make you feel inferior without your consent."

What did she mean by that? Well, we all know what it means to feel inferior. Even the most confident person in the world felt inferior at some point in their life. Maybe it was when they were young, and they were just learning. Maybe they were comparing themselves to older and more experienced people. But at some point, they experienced the feeling of not being as good at something as someone else.

I know that we have all experienced that feeling. It's natural for us as we grow, gain knowledge, and gain skills to feel like others are better at something that we are. But it is dangerous if we let this extend on into our lives. It's okay to look at a professional athlete and say that person is better at football than me. Where the problem emerges is when we seem to look around us and feel that we are inferior to everyone else! And when this inferiority is not just something like the ability to run fast or kick a ball. It's the feeling that everything we do is wrong. Or that we are ugly. Or that we're stupid. That's the type of inferiority to which Eleanor Roosevelt was referring.

But she made a very valuable point. People can try to make us feel inferior. They can bully us. They can put us down. They can encourage others to say that we are inferior. But at the end of the day, you have the ability to overcome what these people say to you. I know it's a cliché, but there's a whole lot of truth to the old childhood line, "Sticks and stones may break my bones, but words will never hurt me." Words may sting for a while. But a confident person doesn't allow them to make them feel inferior.

How does that relate to you as a Scout? Well, one part of the Scout Oath says that we are to obey the Scout Law. Are we always going to be able to obey every single Scout Law? Probably not. None of us is perfect. When we as Scouts find ourselves breaking or not following the Scout Law, how do we feel? We might feel that we are weak or stupid or not talented enough.

But Eleanor Roosevelt cautioned us against that type of thinking. First, the most obvious thing that you can do to avoid that feeling is to obey the Scout Law as best you can. But on those occasions where you slip, don't allow yourself to simply blame it on your inferiority. Because, ironically, that becomes a crutch. If your logic is that you didn't obey that Scout Law because you are inferior in wisdom, skills, talents, or conscience, you have given yourself an excuse to continue to not obey that Law.

Take ownership of your actions. If you do wrong, don't get down about it. And don't attribute it simply to your inferiority. Learn from the experience. Gain courage to do the right thing. And next time you're tempted to break one of the points of the Scout Law, let your superiority over temptation rule the day!

TO HELP OTHER PEOPLE AT ALL TIMES #1

IGNORING VERSUS IGNORANCE

Margaret Atwood is one of the greatest Canadian authors and poets. She once said: "Ignoring isn't the same as ignorance, you have to work at it."

What exactly did she mean by that? Well, let's look first at ignorance. Ignorance is a lack of knowledge. It can be applied to academics. If we don't know the answer to a question on our test, we can say that it is due to our ignorance. Now, just between you and me, your ignorance of the answer to the question may be that you just weren't listening when your teacher taught you the answer. But it doesn't change the fact that you didn't know the answer.

In life, we might be ignorant of basic social issues. Have you ever sat down to dinner at a nice restaurant and wondered what all those knives, forks, and spoons were for? Using the spoon that's supposed to be used for your soup in order to eat your dessert may be simply because you have never been taught what silverware was used for which course of the meal. That's simple ignorance.

Have you ever said something to someone when you shouldn't have, simply because you didn't have all the facts? If so, your statement may have been made out of ignorance.

So, ignorance can come in lots of forms. But what Margaret Atwood is saying is that ignoring isn't the same as ignorance. We don't really set out to be ignorant about things. We didn't purposely decide to not know the answer to the question on the test. When we get the grade for the test, we definitely wish that we hadn't been ignorant on that topic. We don't purposely sit down to that nice meal planning to be ignorant about which silverware to use. No one wants to be embarrassed. And we definitely don't want to be ignorant about having all of the facts at our disposal when we make an important decision.

But ignoring someone or something is totally different. When you're playing a video game, and your parents come into the room to tell you something important, you make the decision as to whether or not you give them your full attention. You choose to give them your attention or to rudely ignore them.

What if you notice that your friend is struggling? They may be struggling with their academics, their athletics, their social life, or just with life in general. You have a choice. You can choose to help them out or you can choose to ignore them. The choice is yours.

The Scout Oath tells us that we are to help other people at all times. Is ignoring your friends and family being helpful? I don't think so. Are we to help them sometimes and ignore them at others? No. The Scout Oath says we are to help others at all times. There's not much I can do to help you choose the right spoon. But what I can do is to encourage you to not ignore the needs of your friends and family and to help other people at all times.

HELP OTHER PEOPLE #2

IT'S THE LITTLE THINGS THAT MATTER

One of the greatest humanitarians of all time was Mother Teresa. Mother Teresa was a nun. Although she was born in Albania in Europe, she was best known for the work that she did in India. Her ministry was to take in, feed, and heal the poor people she found on the streets. Mother Teresa was so well known for what she did, her name has become practically synonymous with humanitarian efforts to reach out to and help others.

One of the things that Mother Teresa said during her lifetime was: "There are many people who can do big things, but there are very few people who will do the small things."

The irony of this statement is that Mother Teresa is generally considered to have done many big things. But she looked at what she did, not in total, but at each individual act of humanitarianism that she and her fellow nuns performed.

Part of the Scout Oath is to help other people at all times. What can we learn about the actions and words of Mother Teresa that can help us in the pursuit of this goal?

The main message is that, oftentimes, people are looking for that one big action that will make them famous or call attention to themselves. The artist Andy Warhol was famous for saying that everyone would have fifteen minutes of fame. So, in this day and age of internet notoriety, people are trying to do big things which will call attention to themselves and make them memorable. Things that will give them their fifteen minutes of fame.

But despite her fame, Mother Teresa felt like it was not from one big activity, but from the culmination of many individual activities. It's the same for us. A philanthropist, a person who gives large sums of money to charity and other organizations, may get headlines for donating $1 million to a particular cause. Don't get me wrong, that's not bad. When individuals who have achieved great wealth are able to give back money to help people in need, that's a good thing. But if our world relied simply on the giving of rich people to help people, we would be in a lot of trouble. No, the vast majority of help for others comes from unfamous people who give tirelessly of their time and energy.

Unless any of you have $1 million to donate, then I would encourage you to go with the advice of Mother Teresa. Find the many small ways that you can help people. You may not get as much fame or notoriety as the people who put it all out on the internet, or the billionaire who gives millions to charity, but because of your efforts to help people one at a time, our world will be a better place.

PHYSICALLY FIT #1

KEEP FIT AND STAY HEALTHY

In virtually every survey ever taken, the list of the most famous and influential First Ladies almost always puts Eleanor Roosevelt in the top spot. Eleanor Roosevelt was the wife of President Franklin D. Roosevelt. During her husband's administration, Eleanor Roosevelt began to emerge as a proponent of the helpless. But even after her husband's death in 1945, she remained active in social causes through her death in 1962.

Eleanor Roosevelt once said: "Today is the oldest you've ever been, and the youngest you'll ever be again."

Here's another interesting way to look at that. At the moment you were born, you could have been listed in *Guinness World Records*. You were the youngest person in the world! But from that point, you began to grow and to age.

Think about what Eleanor Roosevelt said. Right now, you are the oldest age that you have ever been in your life. But you're also the youngest that you will ever be. Why is that? Because the moment you are born, you begin to age physically. The average person reaches their peak in terms of strength, flexibility, and athleticism at about the age of nineteen. At that point, the human body that has been getting stronger and healthier begins to turn the other direction. The metabolism and the immune system slows down.

I suppose this all could sound a little depressing. But only if you let that be the case. Due to advances in medical science, better eating habits, and more emphasis on exercise, the average number of years that people live has increased over the centuries.

But today, that is counterbalanced by another effect. Unfortunately, the obesity rate has risen dramatically over the last few decades. Why? I suppose the biggest culprit is fast food. Because it's just that, fast, many people are drawn to eating it in ever-increasing amounts. The other effect is what is called a sedentary lifestyle. As more entertainment devices such as televisions, video games, and computers have come out, more and more people find themselves sitting, rather than exercising. Younger people are especially vulnerable, as they are forming their dietary and activity habits.

One of the parts of the Scout Oath is that you are to be physically fit. Well, the things that we have been discussing are exactly what the Oath is about. You have a choice in your diet. I guess you could argue that you have to eat what your parents put on the table. But by and large, mom and dad tend to give you healthy foods. They're not the real problem. The problem is what you eat when you are not sitting at the family dinner table. That's where the temptation to eat the fat, salty, and sweet fast foods comes in. Resist that temptation and focus on the foods that are healthy for you.

And as for your activities, you're already in good company. With their emphasis on hiking, camping, and other outdoor activities, Scouts tend to be in better physical shape than their non-Scout friends. But even Scouts can fall into the temptation to play one more video game rather than getting out and enjoying the outdoors. Don't fall into that trap. Make sure that you focus on being physically fit!

PHYSICALLY FIT #2

MAKING THAT WORKOUT FUN

One of the parts of the Scout Oath is to be physically fit. If your goal in life is to become a professional athlete or to win Olympic gold, it's pretty scary to read the percentage of humans who actually achieve those goals. Let's just face it. Not all of us were cut out to be jocks. But when the Scout Oath tells us to be physically fit, I don't see anything in there about being a top-notch athlete. It simply means to recognize the wonderful body and health that God has provided for us and to do our best to keep it in top-notch condition.

Here's an analogy. No one said that your car has to be able to run in the Indianapolis 500. But you want to keep it running. So, you give it the fuel that it needs. You get the oil changed when you need to. You take it in for a checkup to keep everything in good working condition. Shouldn't you take the same approach for your body?

But if you ask people why they don't work out, the number one reason is that they find it boring. But does it have to be that way?

One of the most interesting stories from Greek mythology is the story of Sisyphus. Sisyphus was caught eavesdropping on the gods, and they became very upset with his actions. So, as punishment, the gods decreed that Sisyphus would have to push a large rock up a steep hill until he reached the top. That sounds bad enough. But they also rigged it so that it could never be achieved. In other words, his punishment was to doom him for eternity.

Sisyphus figured out quickly that he was doomed to never be able to roll the large rock up the hill. He knew that the torture would come, not from his inability to ever achieve the goal, but from the sheer boredom of doing the same thing over and over again. He decided to take a different approach every time he rolled the rock up the hill. One time, he might go as fast as he could. Another time, he might go as slowly as he could. The next time, he might take a completely different route. Another time, he might try to see how graceful he could be as he rolled the rock.

Just like the challenge of Sisyphus, our need to work out and keep our bodies in shape endures all of our lives. But if you assume that you must do the same thing every time, it will get boring. So, change it up. Don't jog the same route every time. Use your jog as an opportunity to see other sites. Try new pieces of equipment. Visit new gyms and places to work out. Nothing says that you have to work out alone or with the same people every time. Change it around. Create games for yourself. When you're lifting forty pounds, imagine you're lifting four hundred pounds and you're going for the gold!

The Scout Oath says that we are to keep ourselves physically fit. It doesn't say how we need to do it. Use your imagination and your creativity to find new and interesting ways to keep yourself in shape.

MENTALLY AWAKE #1

NIELS BOHR'S FINAL EXAM

One of the greatest physicists in history was Niels Bohr. He was one of the most brilliant people of all time, coming up with explanations of many of the physical things we encounter every day.

While a physics student at the University of Copenhagen, Bohr was not very popular with his professors. He was smarter than his teachers and he let it show. So, when it came time for his final exam, his professor tried to make the question as hard as possible. He told Bohr that the exam would consist of only one question. And he had only six minutes to come up with the answer. Here was the question: "Describe how to determine the height of a skyscraper using a barometer."

For five minutes, Bohr sat in silence, his forehead creased in thought. This only made the professor angrier. When the professor pointed out that time was running out, the student replied that he had several extremely relevant answers, but could not decide which to use.

When the six minutes expired and the professor demanded the answer, Bohr replied: "Tie a long piece of string to the barometer, lower it from the roof of the skyscraper to the ground. The length of the string plus the length of the barometer will equal the height of the building."

"Or, you could take a barometer up to the roof of the skyscraper, drop it over the edge and measure the time it takes to reach the ground. Or, if the sun is shining you could measure the height of the barometer, then set it on end and measure the length of its shadow. Then you measure the length of the skyscraper's shadow, and thereafter it is a simple matter of proportional arithmetic.

"If the skyscraper has an outside fire escape, it would be easy to walk up it and mark off the height in barometer lengths. But I'm guessing that the answer that you are looking for is boring and orthodox. You could use the barometer to measure the air pressure on the roof of the skyscraper and on the ground and convert the difference into the difference in height.

But since we are continually being urged to seek new ways of doing things, probably the best way would be to knock on the janitor's door and say: "If you would like a nice new barometer, I will give you this one if you tell me the height of this building."

The professor was absolutely incensed. But, since Bohr had given him the correct answer to the question, along with several other correct answers, he had no choice but to let him pass the exam.

In the Scout Oath, you are told to be mentally awake. What does that mean? Mental, of course, refers to your brain. It deals with how we should use our brain to the fullest. Why awake? Well, awake is the opposite of being asleep. If you are asleep, you aren't thinking. But, if you are mentally awake, you are active, vigorous, and using your brain the way it should be used.

Very few people were as mentally awake as Niels Bohr. For most of us, we struggle with coming up with the right answer, much less being able to know multiple answers to the same question. But, like Niels Bohr, we should always have a hunger to increase our knowledge. That's what it means to be mentally awake.

MENTALLY AWAKE #2

SEEK PROOF, NOT RUMORS

There is an old Asian proverb that says, "Better to see something once than hear about it a thousand times." What exactly does that mean? Well, life is full of rumors and gossip. Think about your average day. How many times did someone tell you something about someone else? How many times did you then turn around and tell that rumor or gossip to someone else? It may have been true. It may have been false. But people just have the overwhelming desire to talk about people.

When people talk about people, it can generally be positive or negative. I'm afraid to say that most of the time when someone tells you something about someone, it's negative. So, what that proverb is saying is that it is better to actually check out the situation than to simply believe what you're told and hear that rumor or gossip over and over again.

If you look at the origin of the word gossip, it comes from the old term "good spiel" or good story. People who spread gossip might think it's a good story. It's inside information. People will stop what they are doing in order to hear it. And it calls attention to the person telling the story. But is it really a good story? Not if it does harm to someone else.

The Scout Oath tells us that we are to be mentally awake. Most of the time that we think about that, we think that it has to do with academics or the pursuit of knowledge. That is an important part of what it may be referring to. We should all strive to increase our knowledge and learn as much about our world as we can. But there's another aspect to being mentally awake. Mental, of course, refers to our brain. It includes the things that we put into our brain and what resides there. To be mentally awake means to be alert and aware of that information.

If we are simply listening to the same rumors and gossip about someone or a situation without lifting a finger to really check it out, it's as if we are mentally asleep. We're simply cruising through the night. You may have heard the statement that somebody keeps telling you the same bad information over and over again in hopes that you finally decide to believe it. That's what happens when you hear gossip and rumors over and over again.

But as a good Scout who is mentally awake, don't just accept something said about someone else as being true. Take the time and effort to investigate. Don't be afraid to approach that person to find out the real story. When it comes to rumor and gossip, don't sleepwalk through life. Be awake. Be alert. Take the initiative to go to the source and find out what is the real situation.

MORALLY STRAIGHT #1

BE CAREFUL WHO YOU HANG OUT WITH

A father said to his daughter, "Here is a car I acquired many years ago. Before I give it to you, go to the used car dealer and tell them I want to sell it and see how much they offer you." The daughter went to the used car lot, returned to her father, and said, "They offered me $1,000 because it looks very worn out." The father said, "Take it to the pawn shop." The daughter went to the pawn shop, returned to her father, and said, "The pawn shop offered $100 because it was a very old car." The father asked his daughter to go to a car club and show them the car. The daughter took the car to the club, returned, and told her father, "Some people in the club offered $100,000 for it since it's a rare and iconic car and sought out after by many."

The father said to his daughter, "The right place values you the right way. If you are not valued, it means you are in the wrong place. Never stay in a place where no one sees your value."

One of the most difficult parts of the Scout Oath to understand is morally straight. The concept of morals can be very difficult to follow. Morals are the code of conduct that you live with and how you lead your life.

What does it mean to be morally straight? The term straight has taken on new connotations since it was originally written into the Boy Scout Oath. In the case of the Scout Oath, straight carries the connotation of keeping yourself on the path that leads toward a positive outcome for your life. Think of it this way. A road can be very winding. It can move from side to side. If we are going from point A to point B, will we get there more quickly if we go in a straight line or wind from side to side? Obviously, we will get there quicker if we go in a straight line.

If we focus our life on a high moral value, and proceed straight toward that objective, we will live a better life than if we allow ourselves to be pulled off course. That's what morally straight means. Determine the moral course that you want your life to take and proceed without distractions straight toward that objective.

But what does that have to do with our story? In life, where we allow ourselves to go can have a strong influence on our morals. As a young person, you have a pretty good idea of the types of places you should go and the people you should hang out with. One of the keys to remaining morally straight is to avoid situations and people who can be a bad influence on your life. But oftentimes, it can be difficult to know who those people are and what those situations are. Just like in the story, one of the dead giveaways is if you find yourself in a situation where people do not value you for who you are. If you find yourself in that situation, run away, run away very fast. Always place yourself in a position where people trust and respect who you are. If you stick to those people in those situations, you'll find it much easier to remain morally straight.

MORALLY STRAIGHT #2

DON'T BE AFRAID TO MAKE THE RIGHT DECISION

Roy T. Bennett is an influential inspirational author. He is best known for his book called *The Light in the Heart*. One of the inspirational quotes that he wrote is the following: "It is difficult to make the right choice if you fear choosing wrongly."

On the surface, you might scratch your head at this piece of advice. You could easily ask, "Why would somebody purposely make the wrong choice? Don't we all always strive to make good choices!"

Unfortunately, that's not always the case. There are cases where choices are obvious. Let's say that you're on a game show. You have to choose the prize behind door number one or door number two. Is the choice obvious? Of course not. A choice like that is simply pure luck.

But when it comes to moral choices, the choice is usually obvious. Some moral choices might be dictated by our religion. We probably have a holy book that provides us with the answer. Or it may come from our upbringing. Our parents have constantly taught us that things like stealing or bullying others are not right. Or it may just come from that little voice inside of us that lets us know when we're doing the wrong thing.

So, if we have all of those standards that have been set for us, why would we make a bad choice? Mr. Bennett has put his finger on the problem. Sometimes, we fear choosing wrongly. Let's take an example. You're out with a group of other teenagers. Someone dares you to do something that you know is wrong. It may be to smoke something or take something that you know is not good for you. It may be conducting an act of vandalism. It may be bullying or doing something wrong to someone else. Deep down in your heart, you know that it is the wrong thing to do. But then they say that famous line, "What are you, chicken?"

It's called peer pressure. And it happens to all of us. We know the right choice. But we fear that if we make that right choice, our friends will make fun of us. Or maybe decide that we are too goody two shoes and that they don't want to be our friends anymore. Or maybe the other kids won't think we are cool.

The Scout Oath tells us that we are to be morally straight. That means that, even if the consequences of making a right choice could be perceived as being bad for us, we still stand our ground and make the right choice. At the moment that you make the right choice, other people might give you a hard time. But at the end of the day, people actually respect those who do the right things more than they do those who fall victim to temptation. Hold your ground. And make the right choices for the right reasons.

BE PREPARED #1

THE WILL TO BE PREPARED

One of the most famous college football coaches of all time was Paul "Bear" Bryant. As the longtime head football coach at the University of Alabama, he won many football games and many national championships.

Coach Bryant once remarked, "It's not the will to win that matters. Everyone has that. It's the will to prepare to win that matters." How many times have you heard about the will to win? In order to succeed, you have to have the will to win.

But think about what Coach Bryant said. It's not the will to win that makes you successful. Everyone has that. When was the last time you heard somebody say, "I sure hope I lose my next match?" Nobody says that. Everybody wants to win. Perhaps some people have the will to win more than others. Stories are told about how competitive Michael Jordan was during his college and professional basketball playing days. Again, any basketball player playing at those levels wants to win. But sometimes, it seems as if Michael Jordan wanted to win more than everybody else. For example, he was famous for always wanting to have the basketball in his hands when the game was on the line. Michael Jordan would often say that it wasn't so much that he wanted to win, but that he just hated to lose. Regardless of which way you look at, he definitely had the will to win.

But again, everyone in some form or another has the will to win. Now you may say that you have seen someone who was very pessimistic. They might say something like, "I never seem to win." Or, "Every time I play the game, I lose." This is definitely pessimistic thinking. And with that attitude, it would be tough for that person to win. But does that mean that they don't want to win? No. They still want to win, they just aren't putting themselves in the best position to do so by having so many negative thoughts.

Which brings us back to the quote from Coach Bryant. His point was that we can't simply stop with the will to win. Everybody has that. So, what is a huge factor that separates the winners from the losers? The winners are the ones who have prepared themselves to win. Coach Bryant's football players who spent the most time in the weight room, spent the most time watching film of the opposing team, and spent the most time and effort in practice preparing for the game had the best chance of winning the game.

There's another way to say the same thing. You may have heard the statement, "The more I practice, the luckier I get." Well, it isn't luck that causes that player to win the game. It's the practice that gives them a better chance to win. Our Scout motto is to be prepared. That could apply to athletics, like Coach Bryant was talking about. But it also applies to our school, our jobs, our families, and everything that we do. The more you as a Scout go into situations properly prepared, the more successful you're going to be.

BE PREPARED #2

THE BEST WAY TO ACHIEVE YOUR GOALS

One of the greatest French writers of all time was Antoine de Saint-Exupéry (pronounced ghu-per-e). You have probably heard of one of his books, *The Little Prince.* He once said, "A goal without a plan is just a wish."

The Boy Scout motto is be prepared. If you think about it, the motto could have two totally different meanings. The first meaning could be that we should be prepared for a variety of outcomes. As we go into different situations, we often do not know which direction they may go. For example, let's say that you are studying for a test in math. During the time period in which you are being tested, you've learned a lot of different mathematical information. So, you don't know which questions the teacher is going to ask. What is the solution? To be prepared! In other words, be prepared for anything that could be on the test.

That's the real objective for the test. The teacher doesn't want to know if you know certain parts of what have been taught. They want to know that you have mastered all of the things that you've been taught. Therefore, tests are designed with a bit of uncertainty so that you have to study all of the material, and thus, be prepared for anything that is asked.

But be prepared can have another meaning. It could mean that if you are going to undertake something, rather than just rush right into it, you should prepare yourself in order to achieve the best possible outcome. This is the advice that Antoine de Saint-Exupéry had in mind in his quote.

We all know what goals are. Those are things that we would like to achieve. In watching soccer, we all love to hear the announcers shout out "Goal." It's fun to hear the way they stretch it out. Why do they call the score a goal? Because, the goal was the objective that the player set. When they score, they have achieved their goal.

As we all know, the best way for a soccer player to become as good as possible, and to score lots of goals, is for them to have good preparation. Well, the same is true with life. Experts point out that those people who were the most successful in life are the ones who set goals for themselves. Someone once said, "It's hard to know when you get to your destination if you didn't know where you were going." So, you would never set out on a long trip without planning where you want to go. Why should it be any different in life?

If we don't set goals for what we want to achieve, how will we know we have achieved them? So, as part of your motto to be prepared, make sure you set good, aggressive, but achievable goals for yourself. And then develop a plan to achieve those goals. Prepare, prepare, prepare.

DO A GOOD TURN DAILY #1

DAILY MEANS EVERY DAY

The Scout slogan is do a good turn daily. I think we all know what it means to do a good turn. We may not use that particular terminology nowadays. Remember, it was written over one hundred years ago! Today, we might say something like, "Help out everybody that you can."

But I think it's the part about doing it daily that might throw us for a loop. Some of you might think, "Well, I don't think we literally have to do it every single day. It just means that we are supposed to do it as often as we can." You might be right about that. But here's an interesting way to think about it. As often as you come across other people, if you took every opportunity you had to do something good for someone else, would you really have any trouble doing it at least once a day?

So, the real issue is not trying to force a particular frequency on our actions. The real issue is that we frequently have opportunities to serve other people which we simply don't take advantage of. Let me illustrate.

One of the most famous generals of all time was General Douglas MacArthur. During World War II, his troops in the Philippines were totally overrun by the Japanese forces. But as he retreated, he made the famous statement: "I will return."

And he did, returning later in the war to retake the Philippines and ultimately be chosen to accept the Japanese surrender.

General MacArthur once said, "The history of failure in war can almost be summed up in two words, too late." Another military adage says that the successful commander is the one who, "Gets there first, with the most." That's good advice for fighting a battle, but what does it have to do with us doing a good turn?

Well, have you ever had an opportunity to help someone out, but for whatever reason, you didn't do it? It might be that you were a little intimidated by the situation. You might not have been sure what you could do to help. Or, you might've felt that that person didn't want to be bothered at that time. But once that moment is gone, it's lost. Just like the military commander who loses the battle because they acted too late, you've lost that battle because you hesitated.

The next time that you see someone in need, do a quick analysis of the situation. It is wise to ask yourself a question such as, "Am I able to help?" If you encountered someone with an intense medical situation, but you don't have medical training, you could, in fact, make the situation worse. And you will come across situations where the other person wants to be left alone. But frankly, it is more common that that person really does want some help. And, it doesn't hurt to offer. If they don't want your help, they will tell you so. But don't just assume that's the case. When you see someone in need, don't be late. Jump in and see what you can do to help!

DO A GOOD TURN DAILY #2

GRATITUDE

The Scout slogan is do a good turn daily. When you think of that, you might think that it has to be a physical act, such as escorting an older person across the road. But did you know that doing a good turn could also include something that you say to someone else?

Peyton Manning is considered to be one of the greatest NFL quarterbacks of all time. He holds numerous passing records. He was known as an intense competitor. And also, he is considered one of the smartest players to ever play the game.

You would think that the competitors that Peyton Manning played against would remember how effective he was on the field. Or they would remember how he constantly frustrated them with his play calling and physical skills. You would think they would remember his intense competitive drive to beat them on the field.

But in January 2010, ESPN aired a television show providing a biography of Peyton Manning. He had just been named as the Most Valuable Player of the NFL. The story told us something about Peyton Manning that most people didn't know. It was something that Manning had been quietly doing for many, many years. Whenever opponents that he admired retired, he didn't just call them. He didn't just text them. He didn't just reach out to them on social media.

No, instead, Peyton Manning wrote them a personal letter. And he didn't type it! To each of these feared opponents, he wrote a handwritten note, congratulating them on their career and thanking them for their character. When ESPN learned this, they interviewed these opponents. What they found was that, while each had a healthy respect for Peyton Manning's skills, it was that handwritten letter that every one of them mentioned. All of the players expressed their appreciation for this act of kindness and gratitude from one of the greatest players of all time.

I think we all recognize that gratitude is one of the characteristics that we should always display. But did you know that medical research has actually shown that showing gratitude can cause positive medical benefits, not only for you, but for the person who receives the act of gratitude? In this day and age of the focus on me, me, me, people are taken aback when someone thinks of them. When they take time out of their busy lives to thank someone in an act of gratitude, it creates a warm fuzzy feeling.

But the recipient isn't the only one who benefits. We all enjoy seeing the smile on someone's face after we've just paid them a compliment. We feel good that the respect we have for someone else has been communicated and not just bottled up inside of us.

The next time you encounter a situation where your admiration for someone else increases, be like Peyton Manning. If you have a chance to write it down and give it to them, by all means, take it! But a kind word to their face or over the phone, or a text or post can still achieve the same goal. Let them know that you admire them and are thankful for what they have done. Maybe later in life, you can escort them across the street. But for now, doing a good turn can consist of offering up a word of thanks and gratitude.

SEEING IS BELIEVING

Back in 1954, no one had ever run a mile in four minutes or less. It became an infatuation for runners all over the world. The best runners in the world tried and came close. But no one could break the four-minute mile barrier.

But, then, along came a guy named Roger Bannister from England. Roger Bannister wasn't the best runner in the world. In the recent Olympics, he had actually come in fourth in the world. But, although he wasn't the fastest miler in the world, he had something that the others didn't. He "believed" that he could break the impenetrable four-minute barrier.

So, on May 6, 1954, Roger Bannister did what no one before him had done. He ran the mile in three minutes and fifty-nine seconds. Because he believed he could do it, he was able to do it.

But here is the truly amazing thing. Within the next eighteen months, forty-five other runners broke the four-minute mile. All of the runners who didn't believe that they could break a four-minute mile had seen that it could be done. Now they were believers. And that's all it took. Seeing is believing.

How does that apply in your life? If we don't have the athletic ability, running a four-minute mile is probably not something that any of us can do, regardless of how much we believe. But let's take something closer to home. Getting your Eagle rank. Getting your Eagle is hard to do. Nationally, only 4 percent of all Scouts will get their Eagle rank. But what is the main difference between the 4 percent that get their Eagle and the 96 percent of Scouts that don't? The 4 percent BELIEVE that they can get their Eagle.

You may be thinking that you just don't have what it takes to get your Eagle. But look around at those Eagles. Are they smarter than you? Not necessarily. Are they more athletic than you? Not necessarily. Are they better looking than you? Well, that may be the case. But I don't think that helped them out a whole lot. What did they do to earn their Eagle rank? They focused on their goal and believed that they could do it.

But now, you are like the other four-minute mile runners. They saw that it could be done. And they did it. You have seen that earning your Eagle can be done. So, believe that it can be done and you can do it!

DON'T LOOK BACK, LOOK AHEAD

In one of my previous Scoutmaster minutes, I told you the story of Roger Bannister, the first man to break the four-minute mile. As you might remember, he did it because he believed that he could. But you will also remember that, after others saw that it could be done, they believed that they could do it too. In the next eighteen months, forty-five runners broke this previously unbreakable barrier.

One of these runners was John Landy from Australia. Roger Bannister ran the mile in three minutes and fifty-nine seconds. John Landy ran it in three minutes and fifty-eight seconds. And several months later, the two runners would have a showdown. It occurred at a race in Canada.

The two runners ran neck and neck for most of the race. But in the home stretch of the race, Landy had a slight lead over Bannister. But there is a famous photograph of what Landy did next. If you look closely at that photograph, you see that, instead of looking ahead to the finish line, Landy is looking BACK at Roger Bannister. He was more concerned with what Roger Bannister was doing instead of what he was doing.

Sports experts have estimated that the physical act of turning his head around broke Landy's forward momentum. It slowed him down for the brief moment that Roger Bannister needed to pass him and take the lead. That might be the case.

But I believe that Landy also lost that race because he was more concerned with what someone else was doing than focusing on what he needed to do.

In life, we call that "peer pressure." How many of you have heard that term before? Your peers are your friends, classmates, fellow Scouts … anyone that you come into contact with on a regular basis. Peer pressure is when you do something because your peers are doing it. Or they dare you to do something. It doesn't have to be something wrong. It can be that your peers and friends pressure you into doing the right thing.

But let's be honest. Peer pressure is usually when your peers pressure you into doing something that you shouldn't do. But here's the thing. You don't have to do what they tell you or dare you to do. How do you overcome that pressure? By focusing on what you are doing and not what they are doing. Don't do what John Landy did and turn your head around to see what others are doing. Focus on what you are doing. And focus on doing the right thing.

OPENING A VERY LARGE DOOR

One of the greatest writers of all time was Charles Dickens. Even if you don't know his name, I'm sure you recognize his works. They include *A Tale of Two Cities, Oliver Twist,* and his most famous work, *A Christmas Carol.*

Among the many things that he wrote, one of his most powerful statements was, "A small key can open a very heavy door."

Sometimes, the smallest things can make the biggest impact. It seems like every time we have a national election, you hear about someone who wins by just a very few votes. People say that their vote doesn't matter. Maybe that's true when it's a landslide. But you never can tell. Maybe that one single vote could make the difference in who gets elected.

That's also true in life. We may think that we are just one person among billions and billions of people. And I guess that's true. But our impact in life doesn't have to be earth shattering in order to have an impact. You may have heard the famous statement from artist Andy Warhol. He once said that everyone has their fifteen minutes of fame. It seems like that statement is very true. If you watch the evening news, you might see that someone broke the law. Maybe they robbed a bank. Or maybe they assaulted someone. Their picture might be shown for ten or fifteen seconds. But by the next day, they seem to be forgotten.

On the other hand, celebrities, athletes, and politicians can get into the headlines and stay there for years and years and years. But for all the rest of us, we could be perceived as just one of millions of people. But our actions can make a difference. Let's say that a friend is struggling in their studies. If they don't get help, they may flunk a course. If they do enough of that, they may not be able to get into college. They may not be able to pursue their life's dream.

But let's say that you came along and either offered your assistance or directed them to somewhere where they could get assistance. That one small act could result in them passing the test, passing the course, and being able to pursue the life's goal that they have for themselves. That's just one example of how a small action on our part can, maybe not change the world, but definitely change the people around us. So, the next time you have an opportunity to help someone, don't think that your actions won't make any difference. Think of all the ways that it can, and just do it!

LIFE IN THE REARVIEW MIRROR

One of the greatest golfers who ever played the game is Lee Trevino. Sure, he won quite a few tournaments, but that wasn't the reason that he is considered one of the greatest golfers. Lee Trevino is of Mexican American descent. He was one of the earliest golfers of color to play the game. Through his determination, character, and sense of humor, he motivated many people of color to strive for greatness in the game of golf.

As one of the most humorous golfers ever to play the game, Lee Trevino is noted for many of his quips. One of his most famous was, "The older I get, the better I used to be."

Obviously, what Mr. Trevino meant was that when we look back on our past, we often have a heightened perception of the way things used to be. You've no doubt heard the term "the good old days." It's a known psychological fact that people look back on things that used to be, and most of us remember the good things more than the bad things.

But there can be another issue if we simply look to the past. Have you ever met someone who just seems to dwell on the past and isn't able to get past things of ancient history? For example, they seem to remember everyone who ever slighted or insulted them. They seem to be constantly carrying a grudge.

There's no problem with looking to the past. Historians do it every day. All of us should look to the past to see the lessons that we have learned. But there is a problem when you spend your entire life looking back at the past. Maybe it's the faded sports hero who constantly recites their athletic achievements. Maybe it's the over-the-hill entertainer who spends all of their time trying to convince people that they still "have it." Or it's the grumps that can't let go of the negatives in their life.

If you think about these people, how much desire do you have to be around them? If you're like most people, it's not a whole lot. Instead, don't you find yourself gravitating toward the people who are rooted in the present, but also look forward to the future with a heightened sense of optimism. One optimist once described himself as being the type of person who, "went rowing after Moby Dick with a barrel of tartar sauce." People like optimists. People like others who are able to blow off the indiscretions of the past and focus on the future.

The next time you have a choice between dwelling on the past or looking to the future, cast your gaze over to the future. After all, that's not where you used to be, that's where you're headed!

THERE ARE TWENTY-FOUR HOURS IN THE DAY FOR EVERYONE

Have you ever heard the old joke about how the International Procrastination Association was going to put some tips on how not to procrastinate on their website, but they never got around to it?

Have you ever known someone who just never seems to be able to get anything done? Maybe that describes you? These people seem to have the same amount of intelligence as everyone else. They are just as skilled in academics, sports, or just the game of life as anyone else. But when everybody else reaches the finish line, they are still trying to get out of the starting blocks.

One of the most influential inspirational writers and speakers of all time was Zig Ziglar. Zig Ziglar used to say the following: "Lack of direction, not lack of time, is the problem. We all have twenty-four-hour days."

Think about that for a moment. Whenever you talk to a procrastinator, their excuse is that they just didn't have enough time. Or there aren't enough hours in the day. Or that the amount of time they were given to perform the task was insufficient. But then you look at other people who perform the same task. Did the day suddenly grow a twenty-fifth hour? Did the time allowed to complete the task strangely get larger for them?

No, everyone has the same twenty-four hours in the day. So, how do some people get their tasks accomplished and others don't? A Scoutmaster was at Philmont with his troop. He noticed that all the boys and girls were able to get all of their gear together first thing in the morning and were poised and ready to begin hiking, except for one Scout. Every morning, they had to wait while he finished his preparation. The Scoutmaster noted that the Scout didn't have any more gear than anybody else. He had the same physical skills as the rest of the Scouts. He had the same amount of time to pack up as everybody else.

Maybe it was because the Scoutmaster was tired of having to wait for the Scout. Maybe it was because he got tired of hearing the other Scouts complain about being ready to go, but having to wait. Or maybe it was just pure curiosity. But he decided to observe the Scout. What he saw was a clear lack of focus. The Scout would start packing up one thing, only to switch to something else before that task was completed. He would stop to chat with one of the other Scouts. He would roll up his sleeping bag, only to determine that he didn't like the way it was rolled up. So, he started all over again.

While each of these may have seemed like minor things, they added up. And the extra minutes hung like hours for all of the other Scouts who were waiting on this procrastinator.

If you are facing a task, attack it head-on. It may be tough, but putting it off doesn't make it any easier. The next time you face a large task, analyze the task, figure out the steps you need to take to complete it, and attack the task in an organized and efficient fashion. Don't be the one that the other Scouts are having to wait on!

PERSEVERANCE

There's an old joke that goes like this: "A guy got into a cab in New York City and asked the driver, 'How do you get to Carnegie Hall?' The driver answered, 'Practice, practice, practice.'"

In case you don't get the joke, Carnegie Hall is one of the most famous performance locations in the world. Only the greatest musicians and other performers get to play Carnegie Hall. Obviously, the rider was asking for the directions. But the driver gave him an honest answer. You only get to play at Carnegie Hall if you take the talent that you have, practice and practice to hone your skills, and persevere through all adversity to make yourself into the best person that you can be.

I suppose that the answer to the question, "How do you get to Carnegie Hall?" could be, "Have a whole lot of talent." But, first of all, it wouldn't be as funny. Second, it wouldn't be true. In order to succeed in life, you need a whole lot more than just talent. Many, many talented people have fallen by the wayside. Why?

Well, I believe that one of our former presidents summarized it well. While not generally thought of as one of our most outstanding presidents, Calvin Coolidge did rise to the position known as "the most powerful person in the world." President Coolidge once said something that really summarizes the situation. Known as Silent Cal, he didn't say a lot of things, but he did say the following: "Nothing in this world can take the place of persistence. Nothing is more common than unsuccessful men with talent. Persistence and determination alone are omnipotent."

Have you ever known people with a lot of talent who just seem to squander it? They don't practice their craft. Maybe they feel like it's more important to party than to study for a test. Or to practice their sport. Or to put in the extra hours to go through the chords on the piano.

Don't be the person who wastes their talent. Instead, practice, practice, practice. And when faced with adversity, which makes you want to give up, persevere.

THE GLASS IS HALF FULL

You have probably heard the old analogy about a glass of water that is not filled to its capacity. An optimist looks at the glass and sees the glass as half full. But the pessimist sees the glass as half empty.

What's the definition of an optimist and a pessimist? Well, optimists view failure as something that is within their control. They believe that they can influence what occurs in their life. They believe that things generally turn out in a positive fashion. They dwell on the positive, rather than the negative.

By contrast, pessimists view failure as something outside their control. They believe that circumstances are lined up against them. They believe that other people want them to fail. They are firm believers in Murphy's law, which says, "If something can go wrong, it will."

Let's look at an example of an optimist. Have you ever heard that Thomas Edison invented the light bulb? Well, if you have, somebody was giving you a bad piece of information. The light bulb had actually been invented long before Edison took a look at it. The problem was that the filament in the light bulb burned out too quickly. So, it really wasn't very good for personal or commercial purposes. It would just simply have to be changed too often.

So, Edison set out to find a filament that wouldn't burn out as quickly. He tried over ten thousand different filaments before he finally found one that worked. If you imagine that the filaments had to be prepared, built into the light bulb, and then turned on and observed until they burned out, you can imagine that this process took years and years. It says a lot for Edison's patience. But then his comeback, when asked about it, says a lot about his optimism. When asked what it felt like to fail ten thousand times, Edison responded that he didn't see those as failures. Every filament that burned out was an opportunity to learn something that he didn't already know.

In life, we have the opportunity to be a pessimist or an optimist. My suggestion for having more fun and being more successful in life is to be an optimist. If you fail at something, don't look at it as a failure. Look at it as a learning experience that will help you do better the next time.

THINK OUTSIDE OF THE BOX

I'm betting that all of you have heard of John F. Kennedy. He was one of our most famous presidents. However, not all of you might be familiar with Robert Kennedy. Robert Kennedy was his younger brother. He ran for president, but was assassinated in 1968 before the presidential election. Odds are, he would have been the second Kennedy to become president. One of the things that Robert Kennedy said was, "Some men see things as they are and ask, 'Why?' I dream things that never were and ask, 'Why not?'"

Throughout history, ordinary people have tended to fall into three groups. The first group are the ones who are always questioning the way things are. They never seem to be happy. Do you know someone like that? If you do, they probably aren't one of your best friends. Why? Because they're awful hard to be around!

The second group are people who look around and are simply content with the way things are. I suppose that there's nothing wrong with that. That probably defines most of us. But if you look at the history of the world, it wasn't these people who challenged the way things were and made our lives better through their inventions and other ways to do things.

The third group are the ones who, you guessed it, look around and ask, "Why?" They are constantly asking how we can make things better.

Let's look at an example. Have you ever walked onto an elevator that said it was made by the Otis Elevator Company? If I asked you what Mr. Otis invented, you would probably say the elevator.

That's a good guess, but it's wrong. Elevators have actually been around for centuries. The ancient Greeks had elevators. But the problem with elevators is that they were not very safe. You've all heard the old saying that, "What goes up must come down." People just didn't trust elevators, and for good reason. They were very dangerous. Then, along came Elisha Otis. He was one of the members of the third group. Instead of just accepting elevators with their limitations, he looked at the primitive elevator and asked, "Why can't we make it safer?"

So, what did Mr. Otis do? Why, he invented the elevator brake. As an engineer, he developed the mechanism to make elevators safe. It turns out he was a lousy businessman and wasn't very good at creating a company to take advantage of his new invention. But his son was an excellent businessman, and the Otis Elevator Company was launched.

If it hadn't been for Elisha Otis, you might still be stuck on the ground floor. We can all learn from his curiosity and innovation. Next time you look at something, don't be afraid to think outside the box. Use your imagination. And see if you can come away with a better way to do it.

FOCUS, FOCUS, FOCUS

I'm sure that you have all heard of the North Star. Or if called by its correct name, Polaris. Because it is uniquely situated, Polaris falls almost due north as viewed from almost any direction.

For centuries, navigators have used the stars to determine their location and where they are headed. Compasses are notoriously inaccurate, as the location of the magnetic North Pole has shifted over the years and continues to shift even today.

But Polaris never moves. It is the unchanging beacon upon which all navigation is based. But there are two parts to navigation. First, Polaris must remain totally unchanged over the years. What would happen to a navigator if they were basing their readings on an object that was constantly moving? What would be their odds of ever making the same reading twice? Not very good.

But secondly, whoever is doing the navigation has to do it correctly. Just think about it this way. If an early sailor was trying to sail across the Atlantic Ocean, what would happen if their reading of Polaris was off by just one centimeter? Depending on how far they had to go, they could be off by miles or even hundreds of miles. What is required by the navigator? They must have a complete focus on what it is that they are trying to accomplish.

That's the way it is in life. You can use a sports analogy such as taking your eye off the ball. You can simply say that someone got distracted. You could say that someone just doesn't have their act together.

But in all of these cases, one thing is clear. Instead of focusing in on the task before you, you let yourself become distracted. Maybe you get the initial reading correct, but then you become distracted. Either way, it has the same net effect. You're either going to fall short of the goal that you had in mind, or you are going to end up miles away from your target.

In life, we must be like that ancient navigator. Your Polaris is the goal that you set for yourself. Achievement of that goal depends on an unerring focus on the task at hand. While you may not end up falling off the face of the earth, as many of those ancient navigators feared would happen to them, you'll do a much better job of achieving the goals that you set for yourself.

THE MOST MALIGNED WORD

Perhaps the most maligned word in the world is the word excuse. If you look back at the definition of the word excuse, it is "A reason or explanation put forward to defend or justify a fault or offense." Let's say that something goes wrong in a company. The boss asks for an explanation. One of the workers simply gives a reason or an explanation for what went wrong. The boss responds by saying, "I don't want any excuses." But according to the definition of an excuse, isn't that what the boss asked for?

You see, the word excuse has taken on a negative connotation. It seems like it no longer is simply the explanation of what happened. But it has become an explanation for something that happened when there isn't really a good explanation. In other words, it seems to have entered the realm where an excuse means that there wasn't a good explanation for what happened. Someone must've messed up. Someone must have not performed properly.

And that's unfortunate. Why? Because in any company or business, things are going to go wrong. Throughout your life, you're going to be faced with situations where things do not always go the way they should. In many cases, you will be asked to explain what went wrong. If the assumption is always that somebody messed up, or that people are simply offering excuses for poor performance, that business can never really get to the bottom of what actually happened.

The father of our country, George Washington, had a good grasp on the situation. He once said, "It is better to offer no excuse than a bad one." First, note that President Washington knew that an excuse does not always mean that someone messed up. He draws the difference between a bad excuse and a good excuse. A good excuse or explanation may mean that something simply happened for natural reasons. It doesn't always have to mean that someone messed up.

But what is the advice that President Washington was offering? He was saying that if all you have to offer is a bad excuse, and in fact you just messed up, then don't offer up that bad excuse as your explanation. Simply step up and take ownership of the situation. It's okay to say, "Hey, I just messed up." Sure, once you're out in the working world, you could lose your job for messing up. Hopefully, you'll work for a good and understanding boss who knows that they also messed up when they were your age. And they will give you a second chance. But think about it this way. Whether you offer it up as a bad excuse, or you own up to what you've done, either way, you messed up. If there's a job to be lost, either way, you're going to lose that job. So, do the right thing. Don't offer bad excuses for the mistakes you make. Admit that you made a mistake and figure out a way to never let it happen again.

GIVE CREDIT WHERE CREDIT IS DUE

One of the greatest businessmen of all time was Andrew Carnegie. Utilizing new techniques for making steel stronger, Carnegie started a company called U. S. Steel. Carnegie wasn't perfect. He was a pretty ruthless businessman. But looking back, he revolutionized the way that things are built. He employed many, many people. And later in life, he became a major philanthropist. He gave millions of dollars to education, actually starting his own university. And he gave generously to the cultural arts. He built Carnegie Hall, one of the greatest performing arts venues in the world.

Andrew Carnegie once said, "No man will make a great leader who wants to do it all himself or get all the credit for doing it."

As you get older, and finish up your education, you begin working in your chosen field. Some of you might become athletes. Others might become artists. Others might enter fields such as social work, medicine, or law. But the simple fact of the matter is that, statistically speaking, the majority of you will end up in the business world. Regardless of where you end up, there is one feature that is common to all jobs. There has to be a leader. If you are a football player, it's the quarterback in the huddle. If you become a lawyer, someone within your law firm will be in charge. Social workers have bosses. With a business, it's simple. The business will have an owner, founder, president, CEO, or someone who is in charge. But all the way down through the ranks of the company, you will have heads of divisions, teams, groups, and offices.

As you forge your leadership style, remember the words of Andrew Carnegie. If you are heading up a team, it is important that you get the team to work together. It's very probable that you will have the best knowledge within your group. Most likely, you'll be the most experienced. These things are most likely true, since someone in management decided that you would be the best leader for your team.

But just because you are the most experienced or the most knowledgeable doesn't mean that you have to do it all. Any basketball coach will tell you that the worst player is the one who tries to do everything themselves instead of passing the ball and setting up their fellow players. They even have a statistic for that. It's called an assist. That basketball player may not be the one who made the goal, but if they threw the ball to their open teammate who was then able to make the score, they are credited with an assist.

Another error in leadership that Mr. Carnegie pointed out is the boss who constantly takes credits for the actions of the members of their team. You may have had that happen to you. How demoralizing is it if you work hard and achieve something, only to have your boss take credit for it? How much does that motivate you to want to continue to help the team?

So, as you develop your leadership style, remember to be like that team-oriented basketball player. Look for ways that you can get assists. Look for ways that you can help your fellow team members score. And when they do, pat yourself on the back for the assist, but give them full credit for the score!

GO AFTER YOUR OPPORTUNITIES

I'm sure you've all heard of the Honda Corporation. They produce automobiles, motorcycles, lawn mowers, and many other machines. The founder of Honda was Soichiro Honda. Mr. Honda quoted the Japanese proverb that literally goes, "Raise the sail with your stronger hand."

If any of you have done any sailing, you know that you have to raise the sail and constantly maneuver it in order to take the best advantage of the wind, the waves, etc. Obviously, you can raise the sail with either hand. But what this proverb means is that if you use your stronger, more dominant hand, things will go faster. Things will go smoother due to the greater coordination of your dominant side. If you are a right-handed person, you would most likely throw the baseball with your right hand. Have you ever tried to throw the ball with your left hand? It can be done, but it can be pretty amusing. So, what the proverb is saying is that if you use your dominant hand, things will go better.

How does this proverb apply to our lives, though? The way that Mr. Honda suggested we use the proverb was to analyze what our strengths and weaknesses are. Every military commander, prior to the battle, analyzes what they consider to be the strengths and weaknesses of their opponent. At the same time, they must also analyze the strengths and weaknesses of their own troops. In the optimal situation, the military commander would utilize the strengths of their forces to attack the weaknesses of the opposing forces.

In the game of chess, the chess player is constantly analyzing their strengths and weaknesses and the strengths and weaknesses of their opponents. The football coach does the same thing.

In business, there is a common analysis called a SWOT analysis. SWOT stands for strength, weakness, opportunity, and threat. So, the starting point for a good analysis of a company is to determine what they do best. That's followed up by what are their weaknesses that need to be shored up, what opportunities lie ahead of them, and what are the threats to that company.

In life, we can utilize that proverb also. Analyze what your strengths are as a person. And then utilize those strengths in order to achieve success at every opportunity. But don't forget that you can't be good at everything. Try to identify your weaknesses, and then develop ways to strengthen those weaknesses. You'll know that you've been successful when one day, you realize that what you identified as a weakness in life now moves over into the strength column.

IN ALL THINGS, BE THANKFUL

One of the greatest Native American leaders was Tecumseh. Tecumseh is considered to be one of the greatest Native American leaders not because of his exploits in war, but because of his exploits in peace. Like other leaders who encourage peace such as Mahatma Gandhi and Martin Luther King, Tecumseh led his people during a very trying time. Not only did he lead them, but he encouraged them to do great things. He was a great believer in education.

Tecumseh once said, "When you arise in the morning, give thanks for the food and for the joy of living. If you see no reason for giving thanks, the fault lies only in yourself."

When was the last time that you seriously thought about the things for which you have to be thankful? Maybe it was when you were called upon to say the prayer prior to the Thanksgiving dinner. But outside of that, being thankful is probably not something that you do on a regular occasion. But if you sat down right now and began to compile a list of the things for which you should be thankful, I can guarantee that it would be a long list.

But as Chief Tecumseh said, if your list is not long, who do you have to blame? Sometimes, it seems as if, when given the choice, more people want to be the victim than the victor. They seem to dwell upon all the things that they don't have, rather than the things they do have.

One of the most startling statistics is the measurement of happiness by countries. You may think to yourself, "How do you measure happiness?" Well, different researchers have attempted to do this. They can look at physical measurements such as the quality of education, the number of hospitals, or the number of cultural attractions in each country. Or they can try to use more actual measurements, such as how people in that country measure their optimism on a scale of one to ten.

But regardless of how it's measured, one of the most surprising things from the surveys is that the wealthiest countries tend not to score at the top of the list. Wealthy countries, like the United States, fall farther down the list when measured for "happiness." Instead, some of the poorest nations in the world rank the highest on the happiness of their people. Why? Well, you can attribute it to the negative effects of wealth. The Bible says that, "The pursuit of money is the root of all evil." Other religions call people to humility. Some religions call for people to give away all of their possessions. People who have money tend to want to have more money. This can lead to unhappiness in life.

On the other hand, poor people tend to focus on things like family, relationships, and gratitude for the things that they have. They don't tend to focus on material possessions and all of the things that they don't have.

I would encourage you to partake of the exercise of attempting to write down all the things for which you are thankful. But as Chief Tecumseh said, if there aren't many things about which you're happy, you only have one person to blame. In life, look not toward the things that you don't have, but focus on all the things that you do have.

HONESTY IS THE BEST POLICY

I'm pretty sure that you are all familiar with Mark Twain. After all, he is one of the most famous American authors. Here's your trivia for today. Did you know that Mark Twain was the first author to type his book on a typewriter? Up until that time, all books had to be handwritten. But there was this invention called a typewriter. And Mark Twain decided to give it a try.

Mark Twain once said: "A lie can travel halfway around the world while the truth is putting on its shoes."

What did he mean by that? Well, have you ever noticed that people seem to be more inclined to say bad things about other people than good things? I'm not referring to athletes and celebrities. Fans tend to say only good things about their favorite professional sports star, singer, or actor. But when it comes to people around them, have you noticed that they seem to want to share the negative things quickly. But they are not too inclined to say good things about other people.

Why might that be? The most obvious answer would be jealousy. People are naturally jealous of somebody who is better at something than they are. But it may also be their natural insecurities. If somebody is insecure about their intelligence, looks, athletic abilities, or other things, one of the ways that they cope with it is to try to bring down people who are better in those particular areas.

But for whatever reason, saying negative things, spreading gossip, or bullying other people through the things that you say is not what we should do as Scouts. Obviously, if you observe somebody doing something illegal or harmful to others, you have to report that to an authority figure. But that's not gossip. Gossiping is saying something about someone that's not true, or spreading information that may be true, but just simply doesn't need to be spread around.

Let's say that you find out that your best friend is deathly afraid of clowns. Don't laugh. It's one of the most common fears that people have. But that's a pretty private thing. Even though it's true, is that the type of thing that you need to broadcast to the entire school? No. A good Scout, as well as a good friend, keeps those types of things to yourself.

So, next time you have a chance to broadcast something to others, don't make it something negative. Say the best thing that you can think about someone else to the rest of the world!

DON'T BE THE DRAMA KING OR QUEEN

In almost every ranking that you read about the best college basketball coaches of all time, no doubt one of the top five will be Dean Smith. Dean Smith was the legendary coach of the University of North Carolina. You've probably heard of a guy named Michael Jordan. He's considered to be one of the most recognizable athletes of all time. Well, guess who his college basketball coach was? Yep, Dean Smith.

Dean Smith once said: "If you make every game a life and death proposition, you're going to have problems. For one thing, you'll be dead a lot."

Have you ever noticed how with some people, everything seems to be a matter of life and death? If they haven't gotten a date for the prom six months before the prom takes place, the whole world needs to stop rotating while this urgent situation gets fixed.

Of all the problems in the world, their problems seem to be the biggest. Everyone else needs to drop what they're doing and focus on their problems. In extreme situations, this is called narcissism. It's a mental illness in which a person focuses totally on themselves at the expense of anybody else around them. But even if the situation doesn't rise to the level of a mental illness, it can still be a situation of self-focus. A person can be so focused on themselves that they believe that the issues affecting them are the most critical thing in the world, a matter of life and death. You might have heard the nickname for these types of people. They're called the drama queen or the drama king. Everything in their life is a stage production that we all need to be watching.

There are numerous reasons why having this type of attitude can be a problem. First of all, it's tough to be around people whose entire life focuses on themselves. But secondly, when you're totally focused on yourself, who are you not focused on? That's right. You are not focused on your friends, your family, your schoolmates, your fellow athletes, and everybody else around you. As a Scout, we are told to be helpful. It's very difficult to help and serve your fellow person if you're constantly battling your own life and death situations.

Try to put your life in context. If something bad is happening to you, odds are good that it is probably not the biggest thing going on in the world at that point. Analyze the situation, figure out a way to resolve it, list the resources that you need to fix the problem, and get it done. Then, utilize the time that it takes to focus on those around you and figure out how you can make the world a better place!

HOW HIGH DO YOU BOUNCE?

If you mention cranberries, you'll generally get a very diverse reaction. Some people really like cranberries. But others don't list them at the top of their food list. Regardless of how you feel about cranberries, though, the way that cranberries are harvested is quite unusual.

Cranberries are grown in huge watery fields called bogs. Once the cranberries are harvested, they are placed on a belt that runs them up an incline. The cranberries drop from the top of the incline and bounce on a board. How the cranberry is used is determined by how high it bounces! The softest, mushiest cranberries are not able to bounce over a four-inch bar. Those cranberries are then squeezed, and their juice goes into cranberry juice.

But if the cranberry bounces over the four-inch bar, it is considered to be the best of the cranberries. Those cranberries are destined to end up in cranberry sauce and the beautiful plate of molded cranberry that you see on many Thanksgiving tables.

In life, how high you bounce can be a big determinant of your level of success in life. One of the most famous generals of all time was General George Patton. Although he had a bad habit of saying the wrong things and getting in trouble, he is generally considered as one of the top generals who enabled the Allies to win World War II. General Patton once said: "Success is how high you bounce when you hit bottom."

Let's think about that for just a second. In life, every one of us is going to hit bottom. Maybe not the total bottom. Regardless of how badly you think things are, they could probably get worse. But that's little consolation when you think things are pretty bad.

But the really important thing is how you bounce back from those bad times. Have you ever known people who just seem to wallow in the bad times? With them, the glass is always half-empty. They're pessimistic about everything. They grumble and they complain. But they don't ever seem to do anything to make the situation better. How badly do you want to hang out with someone like that?

We need to look to the example that General Patton gave. Our life needs to be like a trampoline. Remember, with the trampoline, you have to be heading down before you can bounce up! If you're in a bad situation, take a long look at it. What caused it? What factors might cause it to happen in the future? And what do we need to do to get out of it? That's how we bounce back. That's how we go from being down in life to being up in life!

DON'T BE AFRAID TO STRIKE OUT

Even if you're not a baseball fan, you've probably heard of Babe Ruth. A lot of times, athletes may be memorable not because of what they do on the field, but because of their personality. Babe Ruth was a character. He was charismatic, fun, humorous, and always seemed to have a great quote for the newspapers. But the Babe was also a fantastic baseball player. He set the record for most home runs, and kept it for many years.

One of the reasons that Babe Ruth hit 714 home runs in his career was because he wasn't afraid to fail. Babe Ruth once said, "Never let the fear of striking out get in your way." Think about it this way. Even though Babe Ruth hit 714 home runs, he also struck out 1,330 times. Striking out in baseball is one of the most recognized forms of failure. It's humiliating to see the look on the pitcher's face after they throw that deadly curveball that caused you to whiff at nothing but air. Not only have you let yourself down, but you've let your entire team down. When you and I fail, nobody is really keeping track of it. But that strikeout goes on that baseball player's statistics for ever and ever.

If Babe Ruth had been afraid of failure, as exemplified by striking out, he would have probably never gotten into the game. He wouldn't have worked hard to be the best player that he could be, so that he could get up to the plate many times in every game. But the attitude that Babe Ruth took was that it was more important to succeed in life than to spend your time constantly worrying about failing in life.

That's true for us. If we want to be the best that we can be, we're going to have to work hard at it. Working hard means that we're probably going to have more failures than successes. But over time, as we improve, we're going to notice that we seem to be having more successes than failures. Even when we get to the top of our game, are we still going to have failures? Sure, even at his peak, Babe Ruth was still striking out more than he was hitting home runs.

But as the Babe said, don't focus on the failures. Simply see them as learning experiences that help you achieve more successes.

HAPPINESS IS THE KEY TO SUCCESS

Most of you are at the age where you are starting to give thought to what you want to be when you grow up. Oh sure, you did a little bit of that when you were younger. Maybe you decided that you wanted to be a cowboy or a cowgirl. Or maybe you wanted to be a pirate. But there's not much market for cowpokes or pirates anymore. So, your thoughts have to turn to more realistic goals for yourself.

A guy named Albert Schweitzer had some interesting thoughts on this topic. You may not be familiar with Albert Schweitzer. He was a philosopher, theologian, and medical missionary. He is most famous for building an extensive network of hospitals in Africa. While spending time building hospitals in a jungle may not be everyone's idea of a good time, Albert Schweitzer loved it. And the reason he loved it can be summarized in the following quotation: "Success is not the key to happiness. Happiness is the key to success. If you love what you are doing, you will be successful."

Let's think carefully about what Mr. Schweitzer said. In your consideration of your future job, have you ever thought something like, "I think that I will be a doctor because I hear that they make lots of money"? Or, "I want to be a famous singer, so everyone will adore me when I'm up on stage." But what if you don't like being a doctor? What if you don't have the talent to be a famous singer, and you are doomed to spend your time moving from one frustrating experience to another?

So, if you make your primary motivation simply to earn a lot of money, to be famous, or to be adored by millions, you may not be setting yourself up for a life of happiness. For example, have you ever wondered why so many famous athletes, actors, and singers end up taking drugs? Maybe it's because all of their success has not provided them with the one thing that they really crave, happiness.

As you formulate your plans for the future, let's follow Dr. Schweitzer's advice. First, determine what makes you happy. Is it helping out people and serving your fellow people? If so, then perhaps a career in social work might be the best job for you. Are you going to make a fortune in social work? No, probably not. But at the end of the day, you'll be much happier with what you're doing. And can you be successful? Sure, you can be the most successful social worker in history! So, focus not on what the world's definition of success might be, but focus your life on what makes you happy.